MASS MIGRATION IN EUROPE: ASSIMILATION, INTEGRATION, AND SECURITY

HEARING

BEFORE THE

SUBCOMMITTEE ON EUROPE, EURASIA, AND EMERGING THREATS

OF THE

COMMITTEE ON FOREIGN AFFAIRS
HOUSE OF REPRESENTATIVES

ONE HUNDRED FIFTEENTH CONGRESS

SECOND SESSION

APRIL 26, 2018

Serial No. 115–123

Printed for the use of the Committee on Foreign Affairs

Available: http://www.foreignaffairs.house.gov/, http://docs.house.gov,
or http://www.gpo.gov/fdsys/

U.S. GOVERNMENT PUBLISHING OFFICE

29–966PDF

WASHINGTON : 2018

C O N T E N T S

Page

WITNESSES

LETTERS, STATEMENTS, ETC., SUBMITTED FOR THE HEARING

APPENDIX

MASS MIGRATION IN EUROPE: ASSIMILATION, INTEGRATION, AND SECURITY

THURSDAY, APRIL 26, 2018

House of Representatives,
Subcommittee on Europe, Eurasia, and Emerging Threats,
Committee on Foreign Affairs,
Washington, DC.

The subcommittee met, pursuant to notice, at 1 o'clock p.m., in room 2200 Rayburn House Office Building, Hon. Dana Rohrabacher (chairman of the subcommittee) presiding.

Mr. ROHRABACHER. Whereas, I have been informed that the ranking member will be here momentarily and I have been given permission by the staff and by Ms. Kelly, as well, that we can proceed and he will be joining us.

Good afternoon. I call this hearing to order. The subcommittee's topic for this afternoon is mass migration in Europe, its history, the current reality, the consequences of migration and what those consequences mean to the transatlantic relationship.

Let me say that from the start what this hearing is not and it is not and cannot simply be a discussion of recent Syrian refugees going, pouring into Europe. Yes, that is part of the discussion, but it is only one part of the discussion. This is a big topic, one with a history which stretches back decades and in terms of migration perhaps even centuries.

We cannot do justice to the issue or the lives of all the people affected without being respectful of the history of what we are talking about today. In recent history, European demographics began to change dramatically after the Second World War. The continent, depleted of manpower after the war, turned to a guest workers program from Turkey, Morocco, Algeria, and elsewhere. That was for labor to rebuild their countries destroyed during the war. Additionally, as Europe's colonial empires came apart, that too spurred migration from Africa, the Asian Subcontinent, and the Middle East. Both the collapse of the Soviet Union and the implosion of Yugoslavia brought new migrants who sought safety, education, jobs, and being reunited with their families.

In 2015, famine and collapsing economies in the Middle East and Africa, as well as the wars in Syria and in the Middle East, caused a spike in migration bringing more than 1 million people into Europe, some of them fleeing ISIS or some of them just desperate to get away from the horrible conditions in refugee camps. Others came seeking employment and a means to support their families. A small portion of those who entered Europe came with bloody and radical intentions. A very small percentage, very small number of these people were terrorists. That, too, will be part of the discussion.

While the 2015 wave has tapered off, the ramification from that event are still with us today. Politically, it has damaged solidarity within the European Union as some states have rejected the Berlin-Brussels position on geographically redistributing asylum seekers throughout Europe. So it has caused some problems there. And it has also raised sensitive questions about how successful European societies have been at assimilating past groups of immigrants.

It is prudent to ask how can European societies absorb hundreds of thousands, perhaps millions of sub-Saharan Africans and Arabs from the Middle East, many of whom are Muslims and all of whom come from a vastly different culture than the ones found in Europe, especially when reaching Europe is an achievable goal now for so many and the mechanisms to return failed asylum seekers and unlawful economic migrants is woefully insufficient or maybe even nonexistent.

The answers have been clearer and they have been also, however, unnerving to many European populations. From the Brexit vote to the rise of the AfD in Germany, and yes, elections in Hungary and the rhetoric about controlling borders and maintaining cultures and preventing radicalization, all of this has been a constant. For the United States, our European NATO allies are among the most valuable partners we have. Their reduced unity and increased political instability do not serve our interests.

However, this hearing will shed some light on constructive ways that we can approach the challenges that we are talking about.

I will now turn to—Mr. Meeks is not here. Maybe Ms. Kelly, do you have an opening statement? Okay. And we will find a way to mark time until Meeks gets here, but I will instead introduce all of the witnesses.

Starting with number one with Dr. Victor Davis Hanson, a Senior Fellow at Hoover Institution at Stanford University. He is a scholar of classics and military history and having written nearly two dozen books, his latest is a history of the Second World War, a book which is right on my desk ready to be read and it has been there for a couple of weeks I might add waiting for me. I appreciate that you have traveled all the way from California to be with us today and to share with us your understanding of this and put in perspective the history of what we are talking about.

We also have with us Dr. Marta Vrbetic. Now with a name like Rohrabacher, no one ever mispronounces my name, so anyway, we are very happy to have you with us today. You are a Fellow with the Global Europe Program within the Woodrow Wilson Center. Previously, you were an Ambassador or Assistant Professor, that is, of Government at Gallaudet University. And she is an expert on European politics and conflict resolution.

Robin Simcox is a Margaret Thatcher Fellow at the Heritage Foundation. He is widely published and an expert in counterterrorism and counterradicalism and I am happy he is with us today and serving as a witness.

And finally now, I am going to try to pronounce this correctly, too. I have failed so far, but here goes, Wa'el Alzayat. Got it. Okay.

He is the CEO of the Emgage, an organization that advocates for Muslim Americans and he has had a distinguished career at the State Department, serving in the U.S. Embassy in Iraq, the U.S. Mission to the United Nations, and the Department's Syria Outreach Coordinator.

I want to thank all of you for being with us today. Should we proceed? Okay. I would ask the witnesses to summarize your testimony into 5 minutes. Anything you want to say more than that you can put into the record and we will also get to a more extensive dialogue once the questions begin.

So Mr. Simcox?

STATEMENT OF MR. ROBIN SIMCOX, MARGARET THATCHER FELLOW, MARGARET THATCHER CENTER FOR FREEDOM, DAVIS INSTITUTE FOR NATIONAL SECURITY AND FOREIGN POLICY, THE HERITAGE FOUNDATION

Mr. SIMCOX. Chairman Rohrabacher and distinguished members of the subcommittee, thank you for the opportunity to testify here today.

My name is Robin Simcox. I am the Margaret Thatcher Fellow at The Heritage Foundation. The views I express in this testimony are my own and do not represent any official position of The Heritage Foundation.

My goal this afternoon is to highlight some of the challenges Europe will face in the future due to both historic and more recent decisions on mass migration.

First are the security concerns related to recently arrived asylum seekers and refugees. The Islamic State of Iraq and al-Sham or ISIS is known to have infiltrated Europe using the unprecedented refugee flow. This was particularly common in 2015 when Chancellor Merkel opened up Germany's borders. Yet, its ideology has also proven attractive to recent arrivals into Europe who were not previously part of the ISIS orbit.

Forthcoming Heritage research documents the impact of the recent influx of refugees and asylum seekers has had on European security. Since January 2014, either refugees or asylum seekers or those exploiting the migrant routes into Europe have been involved in dozens of separate plots in Europe leading to hundreds of deaths and injuries including that of American citizens. The majority of these plots have direct ties to ISIS.

Furthermore, the plots took place throughout Western Europe, with Germany the number one target. The perpetrators came from a broad variety of countries, but most commonly from Syria. Several individuals even had their asylum applications rejected but were unfortunately not immediately deported and this includes those who carried out vehicular attacks in Berlin and Stockholm.

Second are concerns over the doctrine of state multi-culturalism in Europe. This doctrine accepts that different cultures will live segregated lives with no expectation to integrate, leading to the development of separate, parallel societies with competing laws and customs. In the U.K., for example, there are dozens of sharia councils. They adjudicate on a variety of civil issues, including sharia-compliant financial advice and resolving family disputes. These councils operate legally under British civil law. However, one recent U.K. Government report carried out for the Home Office determined that these councils are encroaching on legal matters outside their purview. This report stated that there are now an estimated 100,000 sharia marriages without state recognition, meaning that women do not have the legal rights they should under U.K. law. Certain sharia councils were also adjudicating on child custody and domestic violence issues. The Home Office report went on to highlight "claims that some Sharia Councils have been supporting the values of extremists, condoning wife-beating, ignoring marital rape and allowing forced marriage"

Thirdly, mass immigration can also adversely affect foreign policy. In January 2014, The Guardian reported that senior officials in the U.K.'s Ministry of Defence had assessed that the reality of "an increasingly multi-cultural Britain" could influence future strategic defense decisions. These Ministry of Defence officials cited worries that British troops had largely been deployed to Muslim-majority countries in recent years, such as Afghanistan and Iraq. There were concerns about deploying troops in the future to countries from which British citizens or their families had historic ties. This was an acknowledgment that U.K. policy could see strategic interests abroad sacrificed for domestic security interests at home. And despite the recent modest contributions to U.S. military actions in Syria, there is nonetheless the possibility of future constraints on the U.S.'s closest allies.

Chairman Rohrabacher, distinguished members of the subcommittee, the humanitarian situation many refugees flee from is, of course, horrific. Syria, especially epitomizes this. Nations wishing to adopt the policy of controlled migration in response is entirely understandable. Furthermore, the concerns I have referred to in Europe do not exist solely because of the most recent inflow. Europe has struggled with integration and domestic security concerns for decades. Yet, the most recent inflow has, unfortunately, exacerbated these problems. As a possible solution, European Governments could more rigorously vet asylum seekers, commit more resources to counterterrorism, be more willing to deport those in Europe illegally and place an expectation on newcomers that they integrate into their new environment and respect core European values.

Thank you for inviting me today and I look forward to your questions.

[The prepared statement of Mr. Simcox follows:]

The
Heritage Foundation

CONGRESSIONAL TESTIMONY

Mass Migration in Europe: Assimilation, Integration, and Security

Testimony before the Subcommittee on Europe, Eurasia and Emerging Threats

Committee on Foreign Affairs

United States House of Representatives

April 26, 2018

Robin Simcox
Margaret Thatcher Fellow
The Heritage Foundation

Chairman Rohrabacher, Ranking Member Meeks and distinguished Members of the Subcommittee, thank you for the opportunity to testify here today.

My name is Robin Simcox. I am Margaret Thatcher Fellow at The Heritage Foundation. The views I express in this testimony are my own and should not be construed as representing any official position of The Heritage Foundation.

My goal this afternoon is to highlight some of the challenges Europe will face in the future due to recent decisions made on mass migration.

First are the security concerns related to asylum seekers and refugees.

The Islamic State of Iraq and al-Sham (ISIS) is known to have infiltrated Europe using the unprecedented refugee flow. Yet its ideology has also proven attractive to recent arrivals who were not previously part of the ISIS orbit.

Forthcoming Heritage research documents the impact that the recent influx of refugees and asylum seekers has had on European security.

Since January 2014, refugees or asylum seekers have been involved in dozens of separate Islamist plots in Europe, leading to scores of deaths and injuries. The majority had direct ties to ISIS.

These plots took place throughout Western Europe, with Germany the target of approximately half. The perpetrators were most commonly from Syria.

Several individuals even had their asylum applications rejected but were, unfortunately, not immediately deported. This includes those who carried out vehicular attacks in Berlin and Stockholm.

Second are concerns over the doctrine of state multiculturalism in Europe. This doctrine accepts that different cultures will live segregated lives with no expectation to integrate, leading to the development of separate, parallel societies with competing laws and customs.

In the U.K., for example, there are dozens of sharia councils. They adjudicate on a variety of civil issues, including sharia-compliant financial advice and resolving family disputes.

These councils operate legally under British civil law. However, one recent U.K. government report carried out for the Home Office determined that these councils are encroaching on legal matters outside their purview.[1]

This report stated that there are now an estimated 100,000 sharia marriages without state recognition, meaning that women do not have the legal rights they should under U.K. law. Certain sharia councils were also adjudicating on child custody and domestic violence issues.

The Home Office report went on to highlight "claims that some Sharia Councils have been supporting the values of extremists, condoning wife-beating, ignoring marital rape and allowing forced marriage."

Third, mass immigration can also adversely affect foreign policy.

In January 2014, *The Guardian* reported that senior officials in the U.K.'s Ministry of Defence had assessed that the reality of "an increasingly multicultural Britain" could influence future strategic defense decisions.

These MOD officials cited worries that British troops had largely been deployed to Muslim-majority countries in recent years, such as Afghanistan and Iraq. There were concerns about deploying troops in the future to countries from which British citizens or their families had historic ties.[2]

This was an acknowledgement that U.K. policy could see strategic interests abroad sacrificed for domestic security interests at home.

Despite the recent modest contributions to U.S. military actions in Syria, there is nonetheless the possibility of future constraints on the U.S.'s closest allies.

Chairman Rohrabacher, distinguished Members of the Subcommittee, the concerns I have referred to do not exist solely because of the most recent inflow. Europe has struggled with integration and domestic security concerns for decades. Yet the most recent inflow has exacerbated these problems.

As a possible solution, European governments could more rigorously vet asylum seekers, be willing to deport those in Europe illegally, and place an expectation on newcomers that they integrate into their new environment and respect core European values.

Thank you for inviting me today and I look forward to your questions.

* * * * * * * * * * * * * * * * *

---

[1] Dame Louise Casey DBE CB, "The Casey Review: A Review into Opportunity and Integration," December 2016, https://assets.publishing.service.gov.uk/government/uploads/system/uploads/attachment_data/file/575973/The_Casey_Review_Report.pdf (accessed April 23, 2018).

[2] Patrick Wintour, "Multicultural Britain Rejecting Foreign Conflict, MoD Admits," *The Guardian*, January 22, 2014, https://www.theguardian.com/uk-news/2014/jan/22/multicultural-britain-foreign-conflict-mod (accessed April 23, 2018).

Individuals 75.3%
Foundations 20.3%
Corporations 1.8%
Program revenue and other income 2.6%

The top five corporate givers provided The Heritage Foundation with 1.0% of its 2016 income. The Heritage Foundation's books are audited annually by the national accounting firm of RSM US, LLP.

Members of The Heritage Foundation staff testify as individuals discussing their own independent research. The views expressed are their own and do not reflect an institutional position for The Heritage Foundation or its board of trustees.

Mr. ROHRABACHER. Dr. Vrbetic.

STATEMENT OF MARTA VRBETIC, PH.D., GLOBAL FELLOW, GLOBAL EUROPE PROGRAM, WOODROW WILSON INTER-NATIONAL CENTER FOR SCHOLARS

Ms. VRBETIC. Chairman Rohrabacher, Ranking Member Meeks, and members of the subcommittee, thank you for inviting me to testify before the House Subcommittee on Europe, Eurasia, and Emerging Threats.

I will be speaking in my own name and the opinions expressed in my testimony should not be understood as reflecting the official views of the Woodrow Wilson International Center for Scholars.

Since I have only 5 minutes, I will go and talk about the most important issues that I find: How European politics is changing, what impact might be on the transatlantic relationship, and if I have time, I will go back to the Balkans and the impact of the migration crisis on the Balkans in 2015.

First of all, as you mentioned, the anti-establishment and far-right parties are gaining ground in Europe, as we have seen the recent electoral victories in Austria, Italy, and Germany. Chancellor Merkel took its centrist conservative party to the left, and some of her supporters defected to the far-right Alternative for Germany, AfD. And with just 13 percent of the national vote, AfD has been able to disrupt German politics, making it more difficult, for example, for Chancellor Merkel to form the new government.

I should also say that Russia has been supporting some far-right politicians in Europe and probably is doing so in order to increase divisions within Europe and upset the established governments.

Recently, the United States, joined by France and the United Kingdom, launched air strikes against Syria. The German Chancellor said the action was appropriate, but didn't join the allies in taking the action due to the opposition at home. Basically, the migration crisis, and everything that followed, left the German Chancellor weaker. And we see here how the transformation of European politics could possibly have impacts on transatlantic relationship.

Furthermore, European leaders are beginning to worry about the possibility of devastating far-right attacks which could potentially radicalize Muslims, provoke more attacks by radicalized immigrants and far-right groups, and lead to the breakdown of law and order. I am referring to the hypothetical scenario developed by the EU Institute for Security Studies, which reflects some of the concerns in Europe right now.

Migration has also become a big source of contention in Europe between the new democracies in the east and their western counterparts, especially over how to reallocate 160,000 asylum seekers from Greece and Italy. The Visegrad Four countries—Hungary, Czech Republic, Slovakia, and Poland—remain opposed. They insist that the EU should protect its borders and prevent migratory pressures, rather than distribute asylum seekers. Germany and West European states insist on solidarity and burden sharing.

Because I have very little time left, I will go to what the United States can do and is doing to help Europe. First of all, the United States and NATO should continue disrupting the smuggling and trafficking across the Mediterranean, thereby also helping protect European borders.

Second, there should be no repetition of the experience we have seen in 2015 when 1 million migrants, virtually unvetted, made it to the heart of Europe. Besides posing security risks, and some of the Paris attackers passed through the refugee shelters of the Balkans, the migration influx was destabilizing the Western Balkans and Southeast Europe, causing lots of quarrels among the countries that are still unstable and still have neighborly disputes.

The United States should also urge Europeans to put their differences aside. Eastern Europeans look up to the United States of America, and we should urge them to end their present quarrels with their Western counterparts. Eastern Europeans should embrace solidarity and accept the need to shape the common asylum policies in Europe. Western Europeans need to stop talking down to Eastern Europeans and be ready to examine their failing integration policies at home.

I am overtime, therefore I will end here, as there will be more opportunity for discussion.

[The prepared statement of Ms. Vrbetic follows:]

Prepared Statement of
Dr. Marta Vrbetic
Wilson Center Global Fellow, Global Europe Program
Woodrow Wilson International Center for Scholars

Testimony before the House Committee on Foreign Affairs
Subcommittee on Europe, Eurasia, and Emerging Threats

"Mass Migration in Europe: The Problems of Assimilation, Integration, and Security
and Their Portents for the Future"

April 26, 2018

Mr. Chairman Rohrabacher, Ranking Member Meeks, and Members of the Subcommittee, thank you for inviting me to testify before the House Subcommittee on Europe, Eurasia, and Emerging Threats on the important and timely topic of migration into Europe. I will be speaking in my own name, and the opinions expressed in my testimony should not be understood as reflecting the views of the Woodrow Wilson International Center for Scholars.

As we have seen from the reports and images of the rescues in the Mediterranean, the European migration crisis has a compelling humanitarian dimension. However, the migration crisis has also brought out concerns pertaining to Europe's security and stability, which are the main topics discussed in this hearing, and to which I will limit my comments. I will share my general thoughts on the European migration crisis and its management, including how the 2015 migration crisis has contributed to the current divisions within Europe, thereby weakening the key partner of the United States.

In 2015, Europe saw its biggest migration crisis since the end of World War II, when the international agencies recorded over one million irregular arrivals across the Mediterranean.[1] Without consulting with other European leaders, in the summer of 2015, Chancellor Angela Merkel waived the EU Dublin rules that require the asylum seekers to apply in the country of their first arrival (i.e., Greece). Germany's humanitarian gesture acted as a pull factor for the Syrians facing dim prospects in the refugee camps in the Middle East. Africans and Asians joined the migration rush to make it to Europe before Germany would close its borders again. The crisis peaked in the fall, with more than 221,000 sea arrivals in the month of October alone. That figure is higher than all the arrivals for the entire preceding year, 2014.[2]

Let me clarify here that, given the mixed nature of the migratory flows, I use the term "migration" and "migrants" as a general term to refer to all those on the move, including refugees, asylum seekers, and irregular economic migrants in search of opportunities.

Most migrants came through the so-called West Balkans Route leading from Greece. With the recent memories of war and still unresolved neighborly disputes, the small Balkan states were often in disagreement how to manage several thousands of new arrivals on a daily basis. Wishing to slow down the migratory influx, Croatia temporarily closed the border crossings with Serbia; Belgrade immediately accused Zagreb of fascism for keeping migrants out. Slovenia built a razor-wire barrier to prevent migrants' irregular crossings from Croatia; Zagreb protested that Ljubljana had raised the fence on Croatia's territory. With population of 4.2 million, Croatia had to process more than 552,000 arrivals in a few months, before the end of 2015.[3] Austria, which was coping with 11,000 new arrivals daily, wanted to send them off to Germany, but Bavaria claimed it could not process more than 50 arrivals per hour.[4]

Germany expected that her southern neighbors, particularly wealthy Austria and Slovenia, would take in some asylum seekers, rather than simply waive them through to Bavaria. However, Germany's neighbors in the South and the East resented Berlin's policy of open borders: the German Chancellor opened Germany to asylum seekers and thereby made the decision that affected the states on the West Balkans Route without consulting these states first. A number of EU states, Germany included, introduced border controls in the Schengen Zone, the area that should be free of such controls to speed up the flow of people and goods across the EU's internal borders.

The mass migration inflows overwhelmed the asylum and social services, leading to housing shortages, budgetary concerns, and political divisions in the countries of destination. Virtually unvetted, the mixed migratory influx posed security risks, allowing radicalized elements to slip into Europe undetected. Some of the attackers responsible for the multiple Paris attacks in November 2015 passed through the temporary refugee shelters in the Balkans. The Paris attacks, for which the Islamic State claimed responsibility, came during the height of the 2015 migration crisis and brought into question the policies of open borders, which allowed the masses of unvetted migrants to reach the heart of Europe.

In March 2016, the European Union reached an agreement with Ankara, which allowed for the return of irregular migrants back to Turkey. In addition, NATO began supporting Frontex, the European Border and Coastguard Agency, with intelligence and surveillance, thereby helping disrupt the criminal networks engaged in smuggling and trafficking in the Mediterranean. With the Balkans Route officially closed, the irregular sea arrivals through Greece and the Balkans declined considerably, but the arrivals increased on other migratory paths across the Mediterranean, leading to Spain and Italy. The irregular sea arrivals to Italy and Spain originate in the countries of North and Sub-Saharan Africa, while the top origin countries for the Greece arrivals are Syria, Iraq, and Afghanistan.[5] The top destination countries have been Germany, Sweden, and other wealthy democracies with generous benefits for asylum seekers.

In 2018, there have been less than 20,000 irregular arrivals along all the routes, with an estimate of 522 migrants dead or missing.[6] The majority of the arrivals are now from Africa. The top origin countries for the irregular sea arrivals are Syria (11%) and Nigeria (10%), followed by Guinea, Ivory Coast, Morocco, Iraq, Bangladesh, Gambia, Eritrea, and Algeria, with men representing 68% of the total arrivals.[7]

To limit the "pull factor" that attracts migrants to Europe, the top destination countries, including Germany and Sweden, introduced restrictive policies, such as curtailing the rights of family reunification. Meanwhile, the EU started applying conditionality to the agreements on the visa regimes and development aid, in order to pressure the countries of origin and transit to restrict migratory flows, host migrant populations, and accept the repatriation of their nationals who are rejected asylum seekers. Furthermore, the EU is working on setting up some limited pathways for safe, legal migration into Europe, and on reforming its asylum system.

European leaders worry about Africa, where a third of the world's youth will live by 2050, and where the economic development never seems to catch up with its demographic growth. Europe is concerned about the "youth bulge" in Africa, where a lack of economic opportunity could lead to increased protests, radicalization, and migratory pressures against Europe.[8] Some also believe that the climate change will produce mass migration waves in future.

It has not been easy for the EU to take restrictive measures to contain migration because the EU prides itself on being a community built on the rule of law, and committed to democracy and human rights. However, given the potentially large numbers of asylum seekers, Europe cannot accept all those who want to come. The EU leaders also believe that, in taking practical approaches to limit migration, they have been containing the rise of the populist and far-right parties at home, and thereby saving liberal democracy in Europe.

Because of the migration crisis, the anti-establishment and Eurosceptic parties have gained ground in Europe and won important victories in the recent European elections, including in Austria, Italy, and Germany. With its migration policy, Chancellor Merkel took its centrist conservative party to the left, and some of her supporters defected to the far right Alternative for Germany (AfD). In the last German elections, AfD won 13 percent of the national vote, creating difficulties for Chancellor Merkel to form the coalition government.

The German Chancellor now must be careful when pursuing certain policies for fear of triggering the opposition criticism. When the United States, joined by France and United Kingdom, launched strikes against Syria, the German Chancellor said the action was appropriate, but did not join the allies in taking the action due to the opposition at home. In other words, the migration crisis has left the German Chancellor weakened. The migration crisis is changing the nature of politics in Europe, and there may be consequences for the Euro-Atlantic partnership.

Russia has also supported some far-right politicians in Europe, possibly for ideological reasons, for Russia considers the far-right movements as part of the global fight against Islamic terrorism.[9] However, Russia also wants to exploit divisions and weaken Europe.

Furthermore, European leaders are beginning to worry about the possibility of devastating far-right attacks, which could potentially radicalize Muslims, provoke more attacks by radicalized immigrants and far right groups, and lead to the breakdown of law and order.[10]

Migration has become a big source of contention in Europe, particularly between the new democracies in the East, and their Western counterparts. The Gallup World Poll shows that the EU is highly divided in attitudes towards migrants. Out of the maximum possible score of 9 on the migrant acceptance index, the average index is 6.73 for Western EU member states, and 2.77 for Central and Eastern Europe.[11]

In September 2015, just as the migration crisis was developing, the EU Justice and Home Affairs Council adopted, by qualified majority, two decisions on relocating 160,000 asylum seekers from the frontier states Greece and Italy to other EU member states.[12] However, the Visegrad 4 countries (V4)—Hungary, Czech Republic, Slovakia, and Poland—have remained opposed to the obligatory quotas for relocating migrants, arguing that such matters should be at the discretion of the national governments. The V4 countries want the EU to protect its outside borders and prevent migratory pressures, rather than distribute the asylum seekers. Meanwhile, Germany and Western European states insist on the humanitarian principles and the importance of solidarity and burden sharing in the EU. The EU Court of Justice upheld the mandatory quotas for relocating asylum seekers within the EU.

Nevertheless, despite the Court's decision and the European Commission's threats to sanction the members that fail to take in the refugees, the V4 countries have remained defiant. The V4 countries now risk losing the EU funds if they do not accept obligatory quotas for migrants' distribution in the EU. The relations also worsened because the conservative, nationalist governments in Hungary and Poland began curtailing the independence of courts and the media. Some EU politicians have urged using the "nuclear option" against Poland and Hungary: the Article 7 infringement procedures for violating the EU's fundamental values could deprive Poland and Hungary of their voting rights.

The V4, like the rest of Central and Eastern Europe, are young democracies. To join the liberal Europe, Eastern and Central European countries went through a period of intensive economic and political reforms, resulting in benefits for their countries overall, but not the benefits distributed equally throughout the respective societies. Therefore, they are vulnerable to the public pressures and populism. Furthermore, it is easier for the new democracies to backslide on the rule of law, as opposed to the established democracies in the West, with long histories of the rule of law and democratic institutions. Furthermore, unlike Western Europe, East Europeans were under the Soviet control, with their freedoms and sovereignty repressed. Therefore, Central and Eastern European countries are more nationalist and concerned about maintaining their sovereignty. They have not had colonies in Africa and Asia, and do not feel the same urgency about helping developing countries as their Western counterparts do.

The V4 are wrong in refusing to participate in the redistribution of migrants from Greece and Italy. However, their opposition also raises some points that Western European democracies should address. Namely, most of the migrants come from the developing countries with Muslim majorities, and much of the opposition in the V4 countries stems from seeing the difficulties that their Western counterparts have had with the homegrown terrorism and with integrating Muslim minorities in their countries. Moreover, according to a recent Eurobarometer survey, 40 % of European citizens believe that the integration of immigrants has not been successful; 38% believe that the immigration originating outside the EU is more of a problem than an opportunity, while 31% see it as equally a problem and an opportunity.[13]

According to the Pew Research Center, the V4 countries have few Muslim minorities, less than 0.5% of the total population in the respective countries. Many of the Western European countries generally have higher percentages of the Muslim minorities, above 6%, while France and Sweden have most, 8.8% and 8.1%, respectively. The size of the Muslim population in Europe could more than double by 2050, due to birth rates and immigration.[14]

The strength of the immigrant communities matters because of the tensions inherent in liberal democracies when minorities demand collective, rather than individual, rights. The larger, concentrated minorities insist on their autonomy, and the liberal democracies today embrace toleration and rarely interfere with the cultural practices of the immigrant communities. Pushed to the extreme, toleration in the liberal, multicultural societies usually leads to "the politics of indifference," which in turn can lead to the setting up, in the liberal Western countries, of parallel societies that sometimes embrace illiberal practices, such as forced marriages or the female genital mutilation. Multicultural societies thereby can abandon liberal multiculturalism and become pluralist multicultural societies that lack cohesion and tolerate the illiberal next to the liberal values.

The preferred alternative to pluralist multiculturalism or pluriculturalism sketched above is liberal multiculturalism. The latter assures social cohesion (i.e., diversity in unity), balances minority rights with individual rights, and requires an engaged state rather than the politics of indifference. In this model, minority rights and cultural diversity are interpreted within the liberal-democratic framework.[15]

However, liberal democracies today--in fact, post-liberal states in a crisis--feel uncomfortable being assertive and requiring minorities to embrace the values of the majority cultures.

Assimilation has traditionally been a factor of stability in diverse societies; it has led to the complete dissolution of immigrant identities and their immersion into the respective dominant cultures and societies. However, with the greater awareness of minority rights and globalization, liberal democracies have abandoned assimilation and embraced multiculturalism.

The question today is whether the democracies will insist on maintaining multiculturalism within the liberal democratic framework, which also means placing demands on minorities to integrate and accept the values of the dominant cultures in the liberal democratic societies. Or will democracies opt for the politics of indifference and thus end up accepting the parallel societies under a multicultural pluralist or pluricultural model, which generally results in minorities' having weaker loyalties and ties to the mainstream host societies.

Establishing parallel societies can weaken the participation of minorities in the mainstream society and increase their vulnerability to radicalization. The danger of pluriculturalism is also that the majorities will begin to reject multiculturalism and revert to nationalism, as we are now witnessing in some European societies that have not had a good experience in integrating Muslim minorities, have accepted many refugees in the recent years, and where the far right parties are now on the rise.

Migration will not stop entirely, and Europe needs some migrants because its population, including labor force, is on decline. This situation also calls for stronger integration policies to ensure the inclusion of the new arrivals and the cohesion of the respective societies in Europe.

The size of a migratory influx matters: European democracies will need to limit migration in order to facilitate integration. For example, even big, wealthy Germany has had difficulty in absorbing the large migration wave that came in 2015. Chancellor Merkel has recently announced that, at this time, no Jewish school, kindergarten, or synagogue can be without police protection in Germany.[16] While Anti-Semitism has existed in Germany and Europe prior to the migration crisis, the large influxes of Arab immigrants have led to the increased attacks on the Jewish minorities in Europe. It will take some time to educate new arrivals and see them accept the core German values, including the responsibility for the Holocaust and the importance of the good relationship with Israel.

The European migration crisis is a complex crisis that requires, besides a humanitarian response, economic and political measures in the countries of origin, cooperation with the countries of transit, enforced security of the borders, and the integration of the new arrivals in the host countries. It requires much money, and much international cooperation.

The Unites States is already helping and can help furthermore in several ways.

First, the United States and NATO should continue disrupting the smuggling and trafficking across the Mediterranean, thereby helping protect European borders. The United States must also insist that Europe protects its borders.

Second, there should be no repetition of the migration crisis of 2015, when a million migrants, virtually unvetted, made it into the heart of Europe. Besides posing security risks, the migration influx was destabilizing the states in the Western Balkans and South East Europe. The United States should insist that such crises are also security challenges that impinge on the transatlantic partnership and the security of the United States, rather than allow some European powers to view the migration challenges as humanitarian emergencies only, which was the case in Europe in 2015.

Third, the migration crisis may be out of the headlines right now, but possibly even bigger challenges are looming in Europe's broader neighborhood, in particular Africa and the Middle East. Managing these global challenges will require international cooperation of which the United States should be a part. The looming challenges will not only require a humanitarian response, but also development policies, targeted aid, conditionality to urge reforms in African states and negotiate readmission agreements, and cooperation with countries of origin and transit to manage migration.

Fourth, it is also possible that the management of future challenges in Europe's neighborhood will require the use of military force, and that Europeans will have to rely on the United States. However, as we have seen in Iraq, Afghanistan, Libya, and Syria—the top origin countries for asylum seekers in Europe--we have not had the best experiences when it comes to the use of force or calls for revolution to depose dictators in divided societies lacking the institutions and societal reconciliation. We need to take preventative actions now and demand gradual reforms, using conditionality to extract cooperation, and urging reconciliation to shore up fragile societies, with hope of preventing major breakdowns in future.

Fifth, the United States should urge Europeans to put their differences aside. Eastern Europeans look up to the United States of America, and we should urge them to end their present quarrels with their Western counterparts. Eastern Europeans should embrace solidarity and accept the need to shape the common asylum policies in Europe. Western Europeans need to stop talking down to Eastern Europeans and be ready to examine their failing integration policies at home.

In fact, European migration policy should not be either/or, with some demanding border security, and others demanding solidarity and refugee redistribution across Europe. Instead, both should be part of the migration management, which also helps keep Europe liberal. The migration has been changing the politics in Europe and therefore will be having consequences for the transatlantic relationship.

I believe that the EU will muster strength to overcome the current challenges, because any alternatives would be worse. The breakup of the EU would be a calamity for Eastern Europe, a disaster for Europe as a whole, and bad for the United States. A weak or broken Europe would not be able to integrate the West Balkans, which remains unstable. The Bosnian Serbs, Croats, and Bosniaks (Muslims) disagree on almost everything except one thing: they all want to join the EU. The EU membership would also shift Bosnia's decision-making to the European level, away from the paralysis in the Bosnia institutions. The European integration process offers hope for the still unstable Balkans.

In conclusion, the present political divisions are bad for Europe and for the United States. They also play into the hands of Russia, which wants to see a weaker, divided Europe, and extend its influence in the region. A disunited Europe means a weak partner for the United States.

Thank you.

NOTES

[1] UNHCR, "Operational Portal Refugee Situations: Mediterranean Situation," available from https://data2.unhcr.org/en/situations/Mediterranean, accessed April 24, 2018.

[2] Ibid.

[3] IOM Europe, "Mediterranean Migration Response: Situation Report," December 31, 2015, available from https://www.iom.int/sites/default/files/situation_reports/file/IOM-Europe-Mediterranean-Migration-Response-Situation-Report-31-December-2015.pdf, accessed April 24, 2018. See page 8.

[4] Eric Maurice, "Austria in Border Disputes with Slovenia and Bavaria," *EUobserver*, October 28, 2015, available from https://euobserver.com/migration/130866, accessed April 24, 2018.

[5] IOM, "Migration Flows – Europe: Main Nationalities of Arrival," available from http://migration.iom.int/europe/, accessed April 24, 2018.

[6] UNHCR, "Operational Portal Refugee Situations: Mediterranean Situation," available from https://data2.unhcr.org/en/situations/Mediterranean, accessed April 24, 2018.

[7] Ibid.

[8] Valerie Arnould and Francesco Strazzari, *African Futures: Horizon 2025*, Issue Report No. 37 (September 2017), (Paris: EU Institute for International Security, 2017), pp. 19-23, available from https://www.iss.europa.eu/sites/default/files/EUISSFiles/Report_37_African%20futures_0.pdf, accessed April 24, 2018.

[9] David Chazan, "Russia 'Bought' Marine Le Pen's Support over Crimea," *The Telegraph*, April 4, 2015, available from https://www.telegraph.co.uk/news/worldnews/europe/france/11515835/Russia-bought-Marine-Le-Pens-support-over-Crimea.html, accessed April 24, 2018.

[10] Annelies Pauwels, "What If…Europe is Struck by Right-Wing Terrorism?" in *What if… Conceivable Crises: Unpredictable in 2017, Unmanageable in 2020*, ed. Florence Gaub, Issue Report 34 (June 2017), (Paris: EU Institute for International Security, 2017), pp. 29-31, available from https://www.iss.europa.eu/sites/default/files/EUISSFiles/Report%2034_%20What%20If.pdf, accessed April 24, 2018.

[11] Julie Ray, Anita Pugliese, and Neli Esipova, "EU Most Divided in World on Acceptance of Migrants," *Gallup*, September 6, 2017, available from http://news.gallup.com/poll/217841/divided-world-acceptance-migrants.aspx, accessed April 24, 2018.

[12] UNHCR, "EU Emergency Relocation Mechanism: As of 31 December 2017," available from https://data2.unhcr.org/en/documents/download/62510, accessed April 24, 2018.

[13] Eurobarometer, "Integration of Immigrants in the European Union: Summary," Special Eurobarometer 469 Survey, April 2018, pp. 13-14, available from https://ec.europa.eu/home-affairs/news/results-special-eurobarometer-integration-immigrants-european-union_en, accessed April 24, 2018.

[14] Conrad Hackett, Philip Connor, Marcin Stonawski, Michaela Potancokova, and others, "Europe's Growing Muslim Population," Pew Research Center, November 29, 2017, available from http://www.pewforum.org/2017/11/29/europes-growing-muslim-population/, accessed April 24, 2018.

[15] For a discussion of assimilation, integration, liberalism, and multiculturalism, including liberal and pluralist multiculturalism, in political philosophy, see Andrew Heywood, *Political Ideologies: An Introduction*, 5th ed. (New York: Palgrave Macmillan, 2012), Sarah Song, "Multiculturalism", *The Stanford Encyclopedia of Philosophy* (Spring 2017 ed.), ed. Edward N. Zalta, available from https://plato.stanford.edu/entries/multiculturalism/, accessed April 24, 2018.

[16] Carlo Angerer, "Merkel Warns of 'Different Type of Anti-Semitism' in Germany," *NBC News*, April 23, 2018, available from https://www.nbcnews.com/news/world/merkel-warns-different-type-anti-semitism-germany-n868271, accessed April 24, 2018.

Mr. ROHRABACHER. Thank you.

STATEMENT OF VICTOR DAVIS HANSON, PH.D., MARTIN AND ILLIE ANDERSON SENIOR FELLOW, HOOVER INSTITUTION, STANFORD UNIVERSITY

Mr. HANSON. Thank you. I will try to summarize very briefly my written statement, Chairman Rohrabacher.

Mr. ROHRABACHER. Pull the microphone a little closer, we are having a little volume problem there.

Mr. HANSON. What we see now is the largest group of potential migrants since World War Two in the displaced persons that were the result of the invasion of Russia in 1941 and the Russian counter offensive. And it is a pool of 60 to 65 million people would like to leave Asia, Africa, or Latin America, so what we have seen is maybe the tip of the iceberg.

There is a commonality that we share in the United States with Europe. It is always, almost always, a non-Western to a Western phenomenon, that is, the former British Commonwealth, the United States, and Europe have a greater propensity for consensual government, free market economics, transparency in the judiciary and that attracts people who want to enjoy that atmosphere.

Most of the people who are arriving, unfortunately, are coming under illegal auspices. They tend to not have language fluency in the host country in which they arrive. They are not often a diverse group of people. They tend to be concentrated from a particular country or region and they are coming, as I said, in unprecedented numbers. They cause a lot of political ramifications for the host country. Politically, the divide is often progressives who are at least stereotyped to be more sympathetic to social welfare programs or more sympathetic versus conservatives that are worried about tradition, customs and are more skeptical. But more importantly, there is a class divide. The elites who tend to favor open borders, if I could use that term, through their influence and power, are often immune from the ramifications of their own ideology. And the lower and middle class native citizens deal with the problems first hand and that has caused a rise in populist movements, both left and right in Europe and the United States.

There is also a little bit of chauvinism on their arrival because the demography is much more fertile, sometimes three to four replacement numbers rather than 1.4 or 0.5 in Europe or not even 2 in the United States and that tends to suggest that you hear this term demography is destiny and it is a very Orwellian situation where the arrival starts to dictate to the host that they are the future of the country.

Let me just quickly say we in the United States are very fortunate because we have about twice the number of migrants. We have double the percentage of non-native born, but we have a much stronger tradition of the melting pot. Americans are racially, ethnically, and religiously diverse. You cannot identify an American by his appearance in the way that Austrians or Greeks are.

We have a country. Europe is a confederation. And the Schengen Agreement, area agreement, the Dublin, are not as successful in creating a uniform approach to the problem. We have one border that is porous. Europe has many borders, eastern and southern, land and sea, as anybody who has been to the Dodecanese islands and seen what is happening.

We, in America, most of the people who come in have the same faith as the host population, Christianity. That is not true in Europe with the Islamist difference and disconnect. People arriving to Europe are more inordinately male. They are about 65 percent. Ours are about 55 percent. Males, historically, are the root of most problems, especially the younger they are.

Let me just conclude by suggesting there are strategic ramifications for the United States that we often—and I don't want to repeat what Mr. Simcox so eloquently pointed out which I am in agreement with, but NATO is no longer using a draft. Only two countries are left. It is a volunteer army. Experience shows usually when you have a volunteer army, people from the newer-arriving classes are the less economically successful will join the military and that will have a larger number of immigrants.

Secondly, only six countries in Europe are meeting their 2 percent goals of GDP and with this increased social cost, whether it is actual or psychological, they will be more reluctant to meet their commitments.

Germany has been the historic leader of Europe and it is really suffering somewhat being discredited after the financial north-south divide in Europe and then the Brexit divide of which in both cases Germany was at the fore. They are creating a great level of animosity, especially from Eastern Europeans who felt that they had been condescended to by German leadership. And I think this has enormous security ramifications for the United States if Germany is not a credible leader of the EU and the EU itself is not able without a stricter political framework to address this. And we really see an EU now cut not in half north-south but in four ways.

And then finally, we have strong ties to Israel and we know now that the level of perceptible anti-Semitism is rising and there has been an out migration to Israel. That has security ramifications to the United States. And that is, I think, mostly a result of incoming arrival. Thank you very much.

[The prepared statement of Mr. Hanson follows:]

Victor Davis Hanson
Martin and Illie Anderson Senior Fellow in Classics and Military History
Hoover Institution, Stanford University

House Committee on Foreign Affairs
Thursday, April 26, 2018
"Mass Migration in Europe: Assimilation, Integration, and Security"

<u>Written Statement:</u>

Immigration into the West

Immigration into the West from non-Western countries is not new. The catalysts behind it, from hopes of finding greater economic opportunity to seeking sanctuary from political violence, are likewise not novel. But what currently is different are both the size of the influxes (variously estimated at over 5 million persons in the last decade into Europe and somewhere over 10 million into the United States) and the apparent inability of Western societies to assimilate and integrate rapidly newcomers—and the risks inherent in such failures. Not since the aftermath of World War II have we seen a pool of 50-60 million potential migrants per year seeking to leave their home countries, largely due to the aftermath of wars in Afghanistan, Iraq, Libya, and Syria, political violence in Africa, and poverty in Africa, Asia, and Latin America.

European and American commonalities

Both Europe and the United States share many of the same immigration affinities. Few westerners migrate to Africa, Asia or Latin America; all three continents are the chief sources of out migration to Europe—especially the Sudan, Afghanistan, and Syria that account for somewhere between 60 and 70 percent of current arrivals. Immigration is increasingly also not diverse. Most immigrants into Europe again are now mostly from the Middle East, Asia, and Africa, Muslim, and overwhelming male. In contrast, Asia, Latin America, and Mexico supply the preponderant number of immigrants into the United States and the proportions are not so overwhelmingly male.

The idea of a "refugee" is now controversial—given the perception that claiming migration is due to political danger at home or economic exploitation is seen a fast track to sanctuary and legal status.

For the most part, large percentages of immigrants arrive into both Europe and the United States *without* acquiring language fluency of the host country, a high school diploma or the equivalent, or legality. Often their arrival prompts enormous political implications, both in altering domestic political realities in consensual societies (e.g., strengthening institutional progressive and social welfare programs and their political supporters, while creating a populist backlash especially among the non-elite), and in attempts by nations to leverage politically the recipients of their former populations (displaying a sudden interest in the human rights status and social welfare of their expatriate populations).

The ensuing controversies over massive immigration in the host countries often preclude accurate data assessment, given politicization of the issue and sheer size of the migration. No one really knows either in Europe or the United States the exact number of immigrants residing illegally in their countries.

Throughout Europe and the United States, conservatives tend to object to massive non-diverse and illegal immigration. Liberals and progressives are more supportive. In both cases the reasons are both philosophical and political. Often arrivals into Europe and the United States bring with them fears of increased violence, whether defined in the American context mostly by gang and cartel threats or in the European instance radical Islamic terrorism. Arrivals often sense that multicultural doctrines reflect a lack of confidence in their hosts about Western traditions and customs, and often there arises a chauvinism that immigrant waves can change the politics, culture, and demography of their hosts in unilateral fashion.

Current pushback and populist movements in both Europe and the United States are fueled by the number and the inability of immigrants to assimilate. In blunt terms, the middle classes believe that their own privileged elite in the abstract encourages massive immigration, either for political, economic, or psycho-sociological reasons, but has the money, privilege, and influence to insulate themselves from the consequences of their own ideology—a reality that falls on the less privileged who must deal with a host of problems on the ground.

Europe's Far Greater Challenges

While immigration in the West shares the above commonalities, *there are also radical differences.* In comparative terms, the 5 million aggregate arrivals into Europe in the last ten years are relatively modest numbers compared to the resident migrant population in the United States, where the percentage of non-native born currently is about double that of Europe (12-13% to 7%).

Yet for a variety of reasons the United States until recently was far better equipped to absorb immigrants than was Europe. Its economy on average has been more robust and its unemployment rates lower. America has had a far stronger record of the melting-pot in assimilating, integrating, and intermarrying arrivals, and its population until recently has been far more racially and ethnically diverse.

In addition, the majority of immigrants into the United States are from either Mexico or Latin America (60-75 percent) and more often share a common religion with their hosts. While the problem of migrants overstaying visas after entering air and sea ports is universal, the American challenge of porous borders is largely confined to its border with Mexico, whereas in Europe migrants have arrived by both sea and land throughout southern and eastern Europe.

The structure of the European Union lacks the political cohesion of the United States, and individual countries are more likely to question and nullify EU immigration and refugee laws, than are states in America—with some notable exceptions—to nullify federal laws. Efforts to build border walls have proved effective in curbing immigration into Greece, Bulgaria, or Hungary, but often without a uniform EU strategy and with the result of pitting one country against the other, only exacerbating preexisting EU tensions over debt and Brexit. Germany in particular, given its predominant economic and political role in Europe, incurs blame from its neighbors for being the driver of massive immigration, worsening existing resentments over past north-south financial bailouts and Brexit. Any solution to European migration lies with Berlin.

Recommendations

The historic components to successful immigration are age-old and time-tried. Immigration that is legal, diverse, moderate, and meritocratic leads to rapid assimilation and enhances the vitality of the host—and should be the goal of any immigration policy. Its antitheses—illegal, monolithic, massive, haphazard, and non-meritocratic immigration—delay integration, spike social welfare costs, cause massive class resentments in the host country, and fuel political instability and factionalism. Rapid technological changes in automation and robotics somewhat lessen reliance on imported unskilled labor; focus on knowledge-based and computer skills increases the desirability of educated immigrants.

Mr. ROHRABACHER. Thank you very much and Mr. Wa'el Alzayat.

STATEMENT OF MR. WA'EL ALZAYAT, CHIEF EXECUTIVE OFFICER, EMGAGE

Mr. ALZAYAT. Chairman Rohrabacher, honorable members, thanks for having me here today. My name is Wa'el Alzayat. I am CEO of Emgage which is a civic education and engagement organization for Muslim and minority communities. As was mentioned earlier, I served for 10 years at the Department of State on Iraq, Syria, and a lot of the other easy to deal with countries that we are all discussing. I served under some incredible diplomats including Ambassador Samantha Power, Ambassador Jim Jeffery in Baghdad twice. And I worked with Ambassador Robert Ford on the very difficult Syrian crisis for 3 years. So I hope what I am sharing with here is understood as my personal professional reflection on what I have seen firsthand.

As has been mentioned, there are approximately 65 million refugees worldwide, the largest since World War Two. And I know we don't want to dwell just on Syria, but it was the Syrian crisis that led to a 40 percent spike after 2011 in that number. And that is a really in term of the annual displacement. And Syrians right now are the largest number of refugees, over 5 million.

And it is important to understand how we got here just very quickly. It was the escape from terrorist organizations, but mainly from the brutality of the Assad regime which was cited by most refugees as the reason for their displacement. Most Syrians I have spoken with and dealt with had no intention of leaving their country and wish they were still there, had they not been literally barrel bombed out of their homes. And we have seen also subjugated to other means of torture including chemical weapons, etcetera, etcetera.

On top of that, it was really the Russian intervention in Syria in 2015 that led to an increase in that displacement on top of the existing displacement. In fact, the same year Russia entered the conflict in Syria, 1.2 million first time asylum seekers applied in Europe, twice the number the year before. So there is a direct correlation there.

So if we are serious about stemming the flow of refugees into Europe, then part of the answer lies in civilian protection in Syria and other countries that are hemorrhaging people. Now with this latest wave of migration, there is completely understandable anxiety. It is normal. The world is shrinking. It feels like it is shrinking. And not always in a good way.

But we need to level set a little bit. When we look at the terrible phenomenon of terrorist strikes and attacks in Europe, the majority have been done actually by European citizens, not by immigrants and not by refugees. In fact, according to my research and I am not an expert in this field, but this is my research, from January 2016 to April 2017, only four asylum seekers, four, were involved in terrorist attacks. Something else is going on here.

Now clearly, the European project has not been as successful in integrating its Muslim refugees and migrants as we have here. That is clear to me. But why? There is a lot of reasons being cited here, but we cannot neglect the institutional discrimination and public sphere and particularly in the job market, combined with strict interpretation of what it means to be a citizen. This has alienated particularly second and third generation children of immigrants who feel disconnected from the only country they know.

But regardless of all of this, European Muslims are very young. Over half is under the age of 30. These are the continent's future. They are engaged and empowered and we know they are already attached to their societies. For example, 76 percent speak the local European language as their native language. Seventy-five percent regularly intermingle with non-Muslims. And they identify with the host country and that identification is increasing over time.

But more importantly, 94 percent said they felt connected to the country they lived in. These are Muslims in Europe. With the new defeat of ISIL on the battlefield, it is more important than ever to distinguish its nihilist ideology. It has to be defeated. But this requires engagement and tolerance rather than demonization and bigotry. It requires trust building between law enforcement and local communities. It requires creating equal opportunity for everyone and requires respect for people regardless of their faith and treating them as equal citizens.

I know much is usually said about the Judeo-Christian values. I can tell you that you can't have Judeo-Christian values with Islamic values. They are inherently the same. They worship the same God and follow the teachings of the same prophets. Perhaps the best model of integration is right here at home where religious freedom is guaranteed by the Constitution and citizens are not asked to choose between their faith and being American.

According to pure research here in 2017, Muslim Americans overwhelming say they are proud to be Americans, believe that hard work generally brings success in this country and are satisfied with the way things are in their own lives, despite 100 percent increase in hate crimes against Muslims since 2014.

I, myself, I am one of those proud Americas who is also an immigrant and a Muslim and a Syrian. It is the belief of the ideals of America where we are judged by what we do rather than the color of our skin that gave me the impetus to become a public servant and the privilege to work on some of our country's most challenging national security issues. I fear those ideals are under assault.

I personally feel that the real challenges, the emerging challenges facing Europe and elsewhere, it is not the refugees or the migrants. It is the willful abandonment of our cherished values of tolerance and equality under the law. I hope we can all work together on resolving some of these real pressing issues together in a constructive manner for the sake of our country, our European allies, and really the world. Thank you.

[The prepared statement of Mr. Alzayat follows:]

CONGRESSIONAL TESTIMONY

Mass Migration in Europe: Assimilation, Integration, and Security

Testimony Before the Foreign Affairs Committee,
Subcommittee on Europe, Eurasia, and Emerging Threats

United States House of Representatives

April 26, 2018

Wa'el Alzayat

Chief Executive Officer

Emgage Foundation, Inc.

A Shared Story

The movement of people across the globe is as old as humanity itself. Whether the exodus out of Africa into Eurasia by *Homo sapiens* 230,000 years ago, or the Puritan migration of the 1600's to the New World, or the displacement caused by the partition of India, humans have always been on the move in their quest for better shelter, food, security, or all of the above. Today, we are discussing yet another chapter of that same story: The movement of mainly Arabs and Africans, mostly Muslim, into Europe. Although this development has caused understandable anxiety in some circles, it is important to place it within the broader context of global migration and to separate the real versus the imaginary.

According to the United Nation's High Commissioner for Refugees (UNHCR), there are over 65 million displaced people in the world, the largest number since World War II. This includes refugees, asylum-seekers, and internally displaced people. Although this number has been steadily rising, it was the outbreak of the Syrian conflict in 2011 that contributed to a 40% increase in that figure. The brutal repression by the Syrian regime, as well as extremist groups such as al-Qaeda and the Islamic State, against civilians, is the main contributor to the displacement of Syrians, and in turn, this latest surge. According to UNHCR, Syrians are now the largest group of refugees in the world at five million and counting. Other top nationalities are Afghans, Iraq, Eritrea, and Somalia, where many are also escaping violence and persecution. In the case of Syrians in particular, most would not have contemplated making the dangerous journey across the Mediterranean or on foot if they were not being barrel-bombed-out of their homes by the government of Bashar al-Assad. But such has been their fate because they dared to seek more rights and dignity from their government.

Most of these refugees, Syrians included, are currently in non-European countries. In fact, developing countries host the largest share of the world's refugees (86% by the end of 2014). The least developed countries alone provided asylum to 25% of refugees worldwide.[1] With neighboring countries Jordan, Lebanon and Turkey absorbing as many as they can, many Syrians have sought shelter and security elsewhere, including in Europe. Still, it was not until 2015 that this situation became a crisis, which appears to have been exasperated by the intervention of Russia in the Syrian conflict and their relentless bombing of major cities, especially Aleppo. According to Eurostat, 1.2 million first-time asylum applications were submitted in European countries in 2015, more than double that of the previous year. Four states (Germany, Hungary, Sweden and Austria) received around two-thirds of the EU's asylum applications in 2015, with Hungary, Sweden and Austria being the top recipients of asylum applications per capita.[2] Therefore, it is clear that addressing the root causes of instability in places such as Syria and elsewhere are required in order to effectively stem the flow of refugees and to potentially allow some to return home.

With this latest wave of migration, legitimate concerns regarding what impact it will have on Europe are being raised. Will these new migrants, many from conflict-prone areas, destabilize

---

[1] "UNHCR Global Trends –Forced Displacement in 2014". UNHCR. 18 June 2015.
[2] "Record number of over 1.2 million first time asylum seekers registered in 2015". EUROSTAT.

Europe? Will they pose a security threat given the apparent increase in terrorist attacks on European soil that coincided with their arrival? And even if these security concerns are addressed, will their very presence begin to change European society, culture, and norms?

Impact of Migration on European Security

The increase in the numbers of refugees and migrants entering Europe appears at first glance to also be matched by an increase in terrorist attacks carried out on European soil. The number of successful terrorist attacks increased from 4 in 2014 to 17 in 2015 and the number of terrorism suspects arrested in EU countries between 2012 and 2016 increased from 395 to 718, according to Europol.[3] However, most of these attacks have been carried out by European citizens, rather than refugees or migrants. In fact, in the period between January 2016 and April 2017, only four asylum-seekers were involved in terrorist incidents, but no actual refugees.[4] Moreover, these attacks appear to have been carried-out either by ISIL operatives or sympathizers in retaliation for European participation in the military campaign against the Islamic State in Syria and the Levant (Counter-ISIL), which began in 2014. Even Turkey, a Muslim-majority country, has suffered a series of horrible attacks, including at Ataturk Airport and a night club that killed almost 300 people, by ISIL operatives.

Despite losing most of their territory in Iraq and Syria, ISIL (and other radical organizations) may continue to plan attacks against European targets either directly or by inspiring others to act in their name. It is this latter scenario, or what is referred to as the "lone wolf" phenomenon, that requires close cooperation between European law enforcement agencies and local communities in order to intervene before it is too late. Moreover, both law enforcement agencies and local communities must work together to tackle the challenge of returning foreign fighter as well as women and children who may have accompanied them abroad. Of the 5,600 foreign fighters who have returned globally, 1,200 have returned to Europe, although none have been reported to have carried out any attacks since their return.[5]

Muslim communities in the West have cooperated with law enforcement agencies in an effort to prevent possible attacks. University of North Carolina sociologist Charles Kurzman looked at post 9/11 cases where the police had identified a Muslim American as a suspected terrorist while sharing where the tip came from. The research revealed that of the 188 cases reviewed, 54 of the individuals were brought to the government's attention by members of the Muslim American community. Although Muslims should not be expected to answer for the actions of others who may share the same faith (just as Christians do not have to answer for the crimes of extremists among them) Muslim Americans were the single largest source of tips identified in Kurzman's study.[6] Certainly, more needs to be done in term of cooperation, but this requires more trust-building with communities of color, rather than continued accusations that they are not

[3] "EU Terrorism Situation and Trend Report (TE-SAT) 2017". EU Terrorism Situation & Trend Report. Europol: 22–28. 2017.
[4] "Europe's Refugee Crisis and the Threat of Terrorism: An Extraordinary Threat?" Danish Institute for International Studies. May, 2017.
[5] Tim Meko, Now that the Islamic State has fallen in Iraq and Syria, where are all its fighters going? Washington Post. Feb 22, 2018.
[6] Charles Kurzman, "Muslim-American Terrorism in 2013". Feb 5, 2014.

cooperating, or even enabling terrorist attacks. These accusations are more likely to have the opposite effect by forcing communities to become more isolated, and therefore, less likely to report suspicious activities.

Another area of concern are single men who have recently migrated. Many of the Syrian men, for example, have traveled to Germany alone and indeed some have struggled to recreate lives let alone attain the same status they once enjoyed. Languishing in refugee camps, detention centers, or on the margins of society does make some vulnerable to crime or radicalization. The answer is not to further demonize them, but rather, to help them find employment, community, and build new lives.

Integration and Social Cohesion

Beyond the security dimension, the arrival of new Muslim migrants and refugees has heightened concerns regarding the impact this would have on liberal European norms and values. Right-wing politicians and media personalities have gone further by warning of the "Islamization" of Europe and "no-go" zones in the UK, where Muslim fundamentalists are threatening the European way of life. But do the facts support such claims?

First, it is perhaps important to address a misconception about Islam—that somehow it is fundamentally incompatible with the Judeo-Christian values of the West. For anyone who has taken an even cursory look at the three Abrahamic religions, it becomes quickly clear that there are no Judeo-Christian values without Muslim values because all three religions are intimately linked in their belief in God and the prophets.

Second, it is important to note that each European country and the experience of Muslims living in that country are different. Still there are important trends that are worth considering. Muslims are a small minority in Europe, accounting for roughly 5% of the population, although that number is projected to increase to between 7% and 14% (depending on the model) by 2050.[7] According to the same report, European Muslims are also young. In 2016, the median age of Muslims in Europe was 30.4 and half of all European Muslims was under the age of 30. A younger population means a demographic that is more likely to integrate and embrace a European identity that is not necessarily at odds with its Muslim one. According to a Bertelsmann Foundation study that looked at the Muslim populations of five countries (UK, Austria, Germany, Switzerland, and France), 76% of second-generation Muslims were speaking the local European language as their native language. The same study also found that 75 percent of European Muslims regularly intermingle with non-Muslims and that interreligious contact as well as identification with the host country increases with each generation. Even more telling, 94% of all those surveyed said that they felt connected to the country where they lived.[8] The likelihood of integration over time is also backed by another study by a lecturer at the University of Manchester who has researched ethnic communities in the UK. According to Maria

---

[7] "Europe's Growing Muslim Population". Pew Research. Nov 29, 2017.
[8] "Muslims in Europe: Integrated but not Accepted?" Bertelsmann Foundation. Aug 2017.

Sobolewska, immigrants are assimilating over time and those who have been in the country for more than seven years are more trusting of political institutions than those who are white.[9]

Another interesting data point worth considering is the lack of a correlation between fear of Muslim refugees and the increase of refugee inflow into European countries. In Germany, which has received more Iraqi and Syrian refugees than any other European country, the perceived threat of refugees is one of the lowest of all other European countries.[10] This could be attributed to the strong position the German government has taken in welcoming refugees and explaining to the public why and how it is implementing the policy. Despite inherent challenges and political risks in welcoming close to a million Syrians, Chancellor Merkel was nevertheless elected to a fourth term.

While the above indices provide a positive indicator of the integration of Muslims in Europe, more challenges remain. In France, job discrimination and a highly regulated labor market disproportionately affect communities of color, especially devout Muslims. Moreover, the ban on the headscarf, as well as other religious attire dissuades French-Muslim women from seeking careers in the public sector. As a former U.S Department of State official, I cannot imagine preventing Americans from serving their government simply because they wear a headscarf or a kippah as mandated by their faith. In the UK, Islam is considered one of the major religions of the country and as such, Muslims have been more able to observe and practice their religion without having to choose between their faith and careers. According to the same Bertelsmann report, British policy has facilitated the civic engagement of Muslims, for example allowing female police officers to wear the headscarf at work. This in turn, increases the attachment of those serving, and in turn their communities, to the state.

Here in the United States, and according to a 2017 Pew Research survey, "Muslim Americans overwhelmingly say they are proud to be Americans, believe that hard work generally brings success in this country and are satisfied with the way things are going in their own lives."[11] And despite a dramatic rise in hate crimes and incidents against Muslims in America since 2014, Muslim Americans continue their embrace of the "American Dream" and the belief in the tenant of religious freedom as enshrined in our Constitution. Rather than be forced to assimilate, Muslim Americans are an integral part of the American social fabric, with over a third representing the African-American community who can trace their roots to the very founding of this nation.

Why the Fear, Why Now?

The sudden surge of new migrants combined with high-profile attacks by ISIL on European soil, has been a boon for populists and fascists who have been looking for an opportunity to challenge the mainstream political systems in their countries. Combined with pre-existing social and

---

[9] Andy Bounds & Chris Tighe. "Manchester attack brings Muslim integration into focus". Financial Times. June 11, 2017.

[10] "Europe's Growing Muslim Population". Pew Research. Nov 29, 2017.

[11] Michael Likpa. "Muslims and Islam: Key findings in the U.S. and around the world". Pew Research. Aug 20, 2017.

economic anxiety, the ingredients have been mixed to produce a truly toxic brew of xenophobia and racism. Beyond the moral imperative to counter these trends, if left unchecked, they can undermine the very foundation of European and American democracy. We now know that social media has been used to stoke sectarian and religious tensions in Europe and in the United States in an effort to divide societies and sow doubt in the hearts of citizens regarding their political and democratic processes and institutions. European countries have closed their borders and rolled-back their commitments to protecting the rights of refugees and migrants, and here at home, we have now banned people based on their religion from coming here. While there are legitimate security concerns that must be addressed, "effective counterterrorism policies respond to real threats, which in turn means responding to real intelligence about threats." But the prohibition on entry to the United States from a number of overwhelmingly Muslim-majority countries is grounded in neither real threats nor real intelligence." These were the words of James Clapper, former Director of National Intelligence.[12] Xenophobic rhetoric and policies that assign blame to entire communities achieve the opposite of their proclaimed objectives. Instead, they deepen divisions, hinder cooperation, and empower radicals.

Beyond the statistics and arguments that I have provided, perhaps the best example of how to deal with the question of immigration is my own story. I am the product of our immigration and public education system, having immigrated to the United States at the age of thirteen 30 years ago with my family from Damascus, Syria to San Jose, California. Programs such as English as a Second Language (ESL) and a tolerant and welcoming environment gave me the opportunity to learn a new language without being judged, and more importantly, to acclimate to a new culture on my own terms. I was never asked to let go of my heritage as a Syrian, or religion as a Muslim. In fact, these identities are celebrated as part of what makes America great. Our diversity and the uniqueness of each citizen of this country is what makes us great. It is the belief in the ideals of America—where we are judged by what we do rather than the color of our skin--that gave me the impetus to eventually become a public servant and work on some of our country's most pressing national security issues.

I fear that these ideals and values are being threatened because of misconceptions as well as intentional distortion. I hope we can all work together to uphold them for the sake of our country, our European allies, and the people of the world.

---

[12] James R. Clapper, Jr., Joshua A. Geltzer and Matthew G. Olsen. "We Worked on Stopping Terrorism. Trump's Travel Ban Fuels it." CNN Online. April 23, 2018.

About Emgage Foundation

Emgage Foundation is a non-partisan, non-for-profit 501C(3) civic education and engagement organization dedicated to increasing the civic engagement of Muslim Americans and minority communities. Emgage is 100% funded by domestic sources including private donors and foundations.

Mr. ROHRABACHER. Well, thank you.

Mr. MEEKS. Thank you, Mr. Chairman. And good afternoon, everyone. I apologize for being a little tardy. I want to thank Chairman Rohrabacher for calling our attention to an on-going concern of ours as we look at Europe from this side of the Atlantic. Large migration flows into Europe including from majority Muslim countries is not a new phenomenon. But let us remember the flows from the Middle East, Turkey in the '50s and the '60s and from the Balkans and Iraq in the '90s. So although I know we will inevitably talk about Chancellor Merkel's decision on Dublin as a pivotal moment, I would like for us to keep in mind the changing nature of European populations throughout the 20th century and earlier. Some facts have changed, but we have been here before.

I also cannot help but comment on our own changing refugee policies here in the United States. As the world rapidly becomes a smaller place where transcontinental threats affect us all, the Trump administration is acting, in my belief, in an incomprehensible manner: By bombing Syria when he sees fit, not solving the problem, and tightening our refugee policy here at home, a policy that I might add has been very successful. Our refugee policies and mechanisms, by the way, can teach other societies, including those in Europe, best practices.

Before we criticize Europe for trying to integrate from refugees from bloody massacres in Syria or often from regions where are directly involved, I suggest we reflect a bit on what it means when we turn away refugees.

Finally, on a personal note, my family came to New York from the South, from South Carolina, in very difficult conditions that I did not quite understand as a young boy growing up. But they were internal migrants, looking for better opportunities for their children and risked a great deal. They had to travel 12 hours from South Carolina to New York. You go 12 hours, you can be almost anyplace else in the world today. And although they were not escaping a conflict zone, I cannot help but think of my family's experience when looking at videos of families at the Hungarian border, for example.

And I understand that not all of these people are refugees. I understand that they may not have the legal rights in Europe and should be turned away after due process, but I cannot stand for treating the traveler, the lost, the impoverished, the naked, as nonhuman, as a disease coming to infect the West. It pains me to see populations in Europe, political groups across Europe, and even some voices here in Congress, treat fleeing migrants, all of whom went through horrendous journeys, as a political tool to scare their populations instead of pragmatically addressing the causes, the difficulties, and the opportunities of the situation at hand which is what we should be doing.

As Europe or the EU grapples with newly-arrived migrants and integrating refugees, I see this as a test of our liberal values. Can our system, the one in which we fought world wars and cold wars to build and protect, treat the individual, regardless of race or creed, as one with equal rights and opportunity. I believe that the United States can be an example of how to successfully integrate new citizens from far away countries with different cultures.

I proudly represent Queens, New York, which is one of the most diverse in all of the United States. And although I know that this may be difficult or uncomfortable for elements of European and American societies to see, I nevertheless believe in our values and institutions as we move forward. Let us look to incorporate the youth and foster future leaders from all walks of life for they will help today's leaders navigate this change.

I look forward questioning and listening to our panelists as we go forward and I think that this is not a new normal. And if we are to protect our values, our way of life, our societies, we have to have these difficult conversations about race, religious, and individual rights in a free society. I welcome this honest dialogue and I hope that our transatlantic ties can only become stronger as we address the issues at hand and address them collectively.

Thank you, Mr. Chairman, I yield back.

Mr. ROHRABACHER. Mr. Cicilline, do you have an opening statement that you would like to put in?

Mr. CICILLINE. Thank you, Mr. Chairman.

Mr. MEEKS. And I can't wait to hear it.

Mr. CICILLINE. I want to thank you, Chairman Rohrabacher and Ranking Member Meeks for holding today's hearing on mass migration, Europe, and security.

Over the past several years, Europe has experienced significant refugee and migrant flows as people have fled conflict and poverty in bordering regions. This population increase, coupled with horrific violent attacks, has led to heightened concerns about terrorism and crime.

As we discuss this important issue, we should take care not to conflate refugees or migrants with terrorists or criminals. The vast majority of refugees who have sought shelter and protection in Europe are running from brutal dictators, fleeing environmental catastrophe, are seeking a home where they can live, contribute, and worship in peace. It is clear to me that the international community must do more to assist those in need while ensuring the safety of all.

I want to thank the witnesses for your testimony about the current efforts under way in Europe, the challenges that they are facing, and ways that the United States can assist our partners there.

I think yesterday we heard from President Macron who identified the necessity of American leadership to shape the 21st century world order and the responsibility to stand up against this tide of authoritarianism and the effort to undermine important democratic institutions that are essential to freedom and justice in our society.

And I want to just conclude by saying I strongly agree with the final witness who just testified that the real challenge that we face is not refugees and migrants. It is the systematic undermining of our democratic institutions and as you said, the willful abandonment of our values of tolerance, equality, and the value and respect of human dignity. So I hope that we will have a discussion that focuses on how we can promote those universal values of human dignity and respect and universal human rights and recognize that we are a nation that is renewed in every generation by immigrants and refugees and the same happens all over the world.

I thank you and I yield back.

Mr. ROHRABACHER. I would like to thank our witnesses and thank members of the subcommittee who joined us today.

I would like to just to get some fundamentals from Dr. Hanson first. Do you see that—you are well known for your analysis of history and a really detailed and in-depth knowledge of this.

Mr. HANSON. We all agree to democratic tolerance and liberal values, but we have to realize that whether we like it or not, that is largely a Western phenomenon that doesn't exist in Africa, or Asia, or Latin America with the same degree it does in Europe and the United States.

So we are appealing to a tradition and that tradition has emphasized that newcomers engage in a brutal bargain. They give up something of their—we don't ask people who arrive here to give up their food or culture or religion, but we do say they have to give us something to be part of the whole, and that is to accept democratic values and tolerance. And we know from historical exempla that assimilation, integration, and intermarriage, and I am speaking as both of my brothers are married to people from Mexico, it only works when immigration is measured, mostly legal, and diverse.

And what we really want to do then is to make Americans, that is number one. Number two is we do have a lot of hate crimes, but unfortunately, in the United States in the last 3 years most of the hate crimes have been of the anti-Semitic nature and many of them have been the greatest perpetrator were second generation Muslim youth. And so what I am trying to get at is that it is not just the first generation immigration. If you look at Fort Hood, if you look at Orlando, if you look at San Bernardino, if you look at the Boston massacre, we who integrate and assimilate people much better than Europe does, have failed to stress the melting pot and the salad bowl has allowed certain zealots to appeal to a second generation who is more vulnerable to separatism and chauvinism than is the first generation, because they grew up with a bounty of the United States or Europe without the struggle and the ordeal of their home country, so it is very important that we stress liberal values of tolerance to the second generation that are much more prone to violence as we see in Europe.

Mr. Alzayat is quite right. It is the second generation. But the second generation is a phenomenon of massive immigration.

Finally, I think all of us agree that we do a much better job with the melting pot, and assimilation, and integration than Europe, but we are not in a position, especially vis-a-vis Europe to dictate how they are going to run their internal affairs. What we need to do is prepare ourselves to react to maybe their mistakes or their successes. And what we are seeing now is that Europe is dividing left and right, east and west, and north and south over immigration. And Vladimir Putin, for example, is championing a chauvinistic view that has wide appeal in Eastern Europe because elites in the EU have been condescending and giving lectures to people about you have to be more tolerant, you have to be more liberal minded. And yet, they themselves are not subject to the ramifications because of their influence and power and wealth. It is the lower middle classes of Eastern and Central Europe that deal firsthand with this and are most vulnerable to propaganda coming from autocracies that say the Europeans don't represent you or it has failed.

So it is a much more complex idea, but the idea that we can give lectures to the Europeans about their French Revolutionary values, it is wonderful that we would try to do that and we should, but in a practical sense, we have to deal with the realities that they may make unfortunate decisions and we have to protect our security interests accordingly.

Mr. ROHRABACHER. I was just informed that an amendment that I was hoping would be discussed before, will be on the floor in 4 minutes, so that is how frustrating this job can be.

Dr. Hanson, thank you for making those points. I wanted to, let me just say, we want America and we love America for its openness and we are hoping that, as Dr. Hanson was indicating, that what we are doing is making Americans out of them rather than having them change those fundamental values that are American and that relates directly to the insistence on some people who are Muslims who are coming here on, and as they are in London, demanding that they have sharia law and that their families be governed under sharia law. I will just let you have a go at refuting that, but isn't that a very legitimate concern when you have a large number of Muslims coming into another country and then suggesting that they have to have the rights that are totally inconsistent with the culture here of how they treat women and how they treat young girls, send them out to be married at a young age, as well as some of the other elements of sharia law that are totally inconsistent with our beliefs of liberty?

Mr. ALZAYAT. Thank you for that question. You know, there is a lot to unpack. I think here is there is the statement that a lot of Muslims there and here want sharia law. Statistically speaking, most Muslims according to most surveys do not want sharia law, first of all, in the countries that they are living in, particularly in Western countries.

Second of all, we need to understand what sharia law is. Sharia law is the body of religious teaching that a devout Muslim may choose to follow in their daily affairs. And now we are talking here about praying, fasting for Ramadan——

Mr. ROHRABACHER. As you know, no one is complaining about that.

Mr. ALZAYAT. But that includes——

Mr. ROHRABACHER. No one is complaining about that. When you are complaining about that are things that go absolutely contrary to what America is supposed to be about.

Mr. ALZAYAT. Correct. But there are no indications or any evidence that Muslims in any place whether in Britain or the United States have insisted on undermining the existing laws or Constitutions and implementing——

Mr. ROHRABACHER. There is no evidence that Muslims in England or here have insisted that their families will be—they will conduct themselves with their young daughters, that they will be able to give them into fixed marriages or there have been actually, what I understand murders of women who have committed adultery. But that doesn't happen?

Mr. ALZAYAT. Of course they happen and they are horrible. But we are talking about most Muslims or a lot of Muslims versus a minority that is extremist and must be dealt with.

Mr. ROHRABACHER. Well, we are dealing with a situation in the modern world. It doesn't take all Muslims. If you have one Muslim who goes like in San Bernardino where you had two Muslim immigrants who murdered all of these social workers.

Mr. ALZAYAT. Same as white supremacists——

Mr. ROHRABACHER. Okay, but the point is they are there and that is impacting them and resulting in this death doesn't mean because they represented only a smaller group of Muslims that we shouldn't understand that there is a psychological part of this whole equation that has led to the death of all these Americans.

And, I might add, leads to situations in London and elsewhere where you have violence or you have activities that are going on that wouldn't go on. You don't have to say most of them want it, but if you just have a certain number of people there that have not—okay, being vetted you say. Well, I guess that is the question. Should we—I am going to give up the floor in 1 minute.

Should we be then vetting people who come from the Islamic world as to what things they——

Mr. ALZAYAT. We should be vetting anybody who would like to come to the United States.

Mr. ROHRABACHER. Okay, right. But that is not what this hearing—this hearing isn't about anybody. This hearing is about how we deal directly with the Islamic migration.

Okay, so when we deal with Islamic migration, do you think that we should vet Muslim would-be immigrants here, and they should be vetted the same in Europe, to make sure that they do not want to conduct various practices?

Mr. ALZAYAT. I think any immigrant to any European or Western country, including the United States, should be vetted to make sure that they have no ties with any illicit groups and do not hold any illicit views. I do. But that should be for anybody.

Mr. ROHRABACHER. So you do believe then that we can ask a Muslim whether or not he or she believes in four wives or some sort of treatment or some sort of punishment of daughters that is differentiated from sons? Do you think that is okay to vet them for that? Deny them——

Mr. ALZAYAT. If it is applied consistently for the applicant, I am fine for it.

Mr. ROHRABACHER. Okay.

Mr. CICILLINE. I wonder if the gentleman would yield? I wonder if you have the same concerns about all of the teachings in the Bible about mixing two kinds of fabrics, about stoning for infidelity, you go through that list. Do we ask Christians whether they should denounce those teachings? Nobody practices those.

Mr. ROHRABACHER. I would suggest that——

Mr. CICILLINE. Great examples, if you Google all of the claims that are in the Bible that people don't actually do today because if you took them literally, cutting off the hand of your spouse, would we make the same inquiry of Christians coming in?

Mr. ROHRABACHER. Christians and Jews and everybody else who tries to come here should be vetted.

Mr. CICILLINE. I think that is what the witness aid.

Mr. ROHRABACHER. But I will suggest that the last time someone like that who is an immigrant from another country who exploded because of their deep faith in Judaism or Christianity, I don't remember any incident right now because where there deaths because of it.

Mr. CICILLINE. Well, I think the witness said that most of the deaths were caused by people who were citizens of the country when they caused the attack. So that is a fact. We ought to rely on some of evidence and not just sort of our own.

Mr. ROHRABACHER. Can I give the time to the ranking member?

Mr. CICILLINE. I yield back. Thank you.

Mr. ROHRABACHER. Mr. Meeks, you have the floor.

Mr. MEEKS. I was going to let David if he had anything else to say. Because the thing I was going to say just about anybody in America immigrated from somewhere other than Native Americans and I know of a group that still exists in America that was responsible for a whole lot of deaths. They are called lynchings. They are called the Ku Klux Klan. These are Christians and they believe in separation and they believe in violence. They have been very violent in this country. They immigrated from somewhere else. And many of them were involved, not all of them, but many of them, they are still involved in the democracy called the United States of America.

And so to—now I don't blame everybody that happens to be Christians and/or white to say that that for minority who believes in those things that means everybody believes that. And I think what Mr. Alzayat is saying is that there is a small minority. You can find a small minority of people of any faith, of any ethnic group that are horrible people, but you don't go after the whole spectrum when the overwhelming majority—because it is human nature to have somebody that is evil. And we want to stop out and make sort of the evil folks don't get in or don't stay here. But that is not because they are not evil because they are Muslim. Just like you don't—they are evil people and we call them who they are.

But Muslims, if you look at the religion, it is a very peaceful religion and that is what they teach and that is how they live by. And for us to color it some other kind of way is not going to resolve issues. It is going to cause issues. And I think that what we are talking about, I mean, the fact of the matter is in the United States previously all you had to do was get here. When you came into Staten Island, you registered, they didn't care, as long as you got here because it says give me your tired, give me your weary, give me, you know, we want you, except for those that were brought over in the hulls of slave ships.

Mr. ROHRABACHER. Do you want to give him a question?

Mr. MEEKS. I am, but you opened the door. I wasn't going that way at all, so there is no way in any good conscience because I sit back and just allow, you know, me and you are good friends, and I often have to come back after you have made a statement, you take me off my game plan and I have got it on automatic because I have got to address it because I don't want the record to indicate that I can allow a statement that I so 180 degree disagree with to stand and to go.

I don't want the record to indicate to anybody that might be listening to this hearing, who might be in this room, or who—this is being recorded, that Gregory Meeks stood by and just allowed the kind of questioning and the statements that were just made to go without hearing my strong opposition to those statements and to what was insinuated here.

Mr. ROHRABACHER. Is that to be interpreted that you don't believe in vetting people for their religious convictions that may be violent and cause——

Mr. MEEKS. I believe in vetting everyone, not just because of their religious beliefs. I think that as a result, I want to make sure—I don't care if you are a Muslim, if you are Jewish, if you are Buddhist, if you are anyone who is going to come here that you are evil and you are coming here to do harm, I want to vet them, but not because you are a Muslim. That is not what makes the reason why, just because you are a Muslim.

There are Christians that commit more crime in America than anyone else. There are more Christians that commit crimes in the United States of America than any other religious belief. There has been more deaths of people of the Christian faith in the United States of America than any other religion. And I am a Christian, but I yield the question to Ms. Kelly.

Mr. ROHRABACHER. You are next, Ms. Kelly. Go right ahead.

Ms. KELLY. Thank you, Mr. Chairman. I do associate myself with the comments of the ranking member, but with the unrest in the Middle East and Russia's invasion of Ukraine, Europe has experienced increased migration flows not seen since the fall of communism. Many European countries have taken in significant numbers of refugees looking for employment and a better way of life.

Many countries, however, have used the increased flows to stoke xenophobic sentiments and push anti-immigration policies. Many of these policies are aimed at Muslim populations, but countries like Poland have taken in a significant number of Ukrainians.

The Polish Government claims to host about 1 million Ukrainian refugees of its territory. Many of these people are migrant workers, in fact, filling the labor demand in a currently well-performing economy. At the same time, there is also tension between the local population and Ukrainians which recalls troubling history between the two nations in the 20th century.

Warsaw touts the fact that they host Ukrainians who are more like the Poles culturally as a reason to not accept Syrians.

I think it is important to note that the migration issue in Europe is not just about Muslim populations. There are many different groups immigrating to Europe, reports of anti-Ukraine job postings reminiscent of the Irish Need Not Apply, are now popping up in new reports out of Poland. And yet, Polish unemployment is low and the immigration wave has delayed Poland's migration aging by years.

Ms. Vrbetic, what type of rights do Ukrainians have when they are entering the EU as migrant workers versus refugees? In interest of full disclosure, my grandmother on my mother's side, they are Ukrainian, so half of my family is.

Ms. VRBETIC. Thank you for your question. I am afraid I wouldn't know about the rights of Ukrainians who enter into Poland. I could research that and get back to you.

I am aware though that yes, Poland has accepted many Ukrainians. Yes, I am aware of that.

Ms. KELLY. Can anyone else answer?

Ms. VRBETIC. I do have some other comments.

Ms. KELLY. Okay.

Ms. VRBETIC. If I could add to this general discussion.

Ms. KELLY. Sure.

Ms. VRBETIC. First of all, and I am making comments as somebody who is an immigrant. Can you hear me? I am trying to speak into the mic now. Someone who is an immigrant, and somebody who was raised and born and Europe. I am a U.S. citizen. I am a minority in several ways, including being completely deaf, and you know, just a minority, lots of things. So I do sympathize with many things that were expressed here. And I think we may be talking past each other.

So let me tell you the reasons why I think that the migration to Europe, that the solution is not just to accept everybody who wants to come. First of all, because there are so many migrants. We are talking about 60 million that might appear at European borders, and when I use the term migrant, I am using it as a general term. It can include asylum seekers. It could include refugees. It could include those who are seeking economic opportunity.

The second thing is, we are talking about the upcoming problems in Africa, where there will be one third of the world's youth by 2050. The youth bulge is usually associated with protests and possibly radicalization. There will be no jobs. There is no way that Europe can absorb all of the people who want to appear on its borders, so this is the reason.

The second——

Ms. KELLY. I know you are—I only have a certain amount of time myself, so I wanted to get another question in.

Ms. VRBETIC. I apologize. The first time in a hearing, so I may not fully know the procedure.

Ms. KELLY. No problem.

Ms. VRBETIC. I apologize.

Ms. KELLY. Mr. Alzayat, I understand that many immigrants to the U.K. come from outside the EU and are not new to the U.K. In fact, we are looking at second or third or fourth generation British citizens or French or Belgian who do not feel like they are fully-fledged Brits. How can we work with the powers that be, the old guard in economics and politics, to open doors and provide equal opportunity to all citizens? This is the tool against radicalization. What success stories have there been if you know of and it seems like we only focus on the negative aspects of all of this.

Mr. ALZAYAT. Thank you for that question. You know, it is clear to me that true social integration requires investment in education and also in employment as the basic ingredients. If you look at France, they actually do a great job in education, but the labor market is overly regulated and inherently discriminatory. So you end up with well-educated minorities with no jobs.

Germany does not have quite the same robust educational system, particularly for minority communities especially in early age,
however—and there are more barriers, especially because of the
language, but a much more lax and welcoming labor market. And
as such, you see big difference in terms of the perception of those
communities of themselves, of the connectiveness to the society and
their success and their income which by the way irrespective of
that, it is still lower actually than the white Europeans.

So really the way forward here is to invest more in education of
these children and providing job opportunities. But another piece
really is in Britain this has been, I think, done in the right way.
Islam needs to be recognized as one of the major religions. And it
needs to be true inclusivity of people who are practicing that religion in the public sphere.

There was a comment made earlier that this fear that the more
Muslims there are in the armed forces of NATO or in the policy
circles, somehow that is going to negatively affect European foreign
policy and engagement abroad. I think the opposite happens. You
have a more committed, civically engaged community that is helping you flesh out these ideas and tackle some very difficult issues
and giving you diversity of opinion and credibility when engaging
with those. And that is my own experience as a representative of
the State Department. I would like to think that people like me
and us actually help our country be stronger when we engage
abroad with people of different faith, color, and religions.

Ms. KELLY. I know I am out of time, but when I listen to you,
I am very big in the gun violence prevention fight and I can apply
what you said to some of our urban areas, the investment and education and employment would make such a difference and more
inclusivity. So thank you.

Mr. ROHRABACHER. I am going to put the subcommittee on recess
for ½ hour. And we will come back and hopefully have—there have
been some very profound statements made. I certainly would like
to hear some comments on them, but we will be back in ½ hour.
This committee is in recess.

[Recess.]

Mr. ROHRABACHER. This hearing is readjourned or unadjourned,
that is it. Reconvened, that is the word I am looking for.

Okay, I have been running back and forth to the floor where I
had an amendment on the floor and it would not have been able
to be brought up unless I was there, and I want to thank all of you
for joining us today and being understanding of this hectic sched-
ule.

We had a very lively discussion and I would like Dr. Hanson and
perhaps Dr. Vrbetic, as well, to have a chance to comment on what
we were saying before. So Dr. Hanson.

Mr. HANSON. I think that we have to be precise in the nomen-
clature when we talk about as was mentioned violence. Violence is
endemic in any society. There is such a thing called politically-motivated violence and the statistics suggest that politically-motivated
violence with an agenda to further a political cause in Europe and
in the United States most of the incidents in the last two decades
or since 9/11 have been so-called Islamic inspired. That is what the
perpetrators have suggested.

Second is that a minority of Muslims are prone to violence, I think that is correct. But when you are working with a pool of 5 million over the last decade that have migrated or you have 1.7 million in Europe, just 1 percent of that pool would be 50,000 people, so that is something to watch. You can be successful in 99 percent of the case, but if you have a group of people who feel alienated from society and are prone to radical Islamic doctrine, that is a large pool, given the European inexperience and inability to assimilate in the fashion that we do.

I think when we talk about hate crimes, we have to be very specific. If you go to the FBI statistics, the group that is most subject to hate crime violence are American Jews in the United States of Jewish faith. At least according to FBI statistics, the group that is most identified with perpetrating those hate crimes are Islamic zealots. So it is not accurate to say that American Jews are not the most—they are the most targeted group, at least according to Federal statistics.

Again, I don't think that the United States, given our long relations with Europe, it is very ironic that Europe is used to lecturing us, but I don't think we are in a position to alter fundamentally European policy. What our prerogative and our duty is to do is to protect us and this question has affected the NATO alliance, especially the southern flank with tensions with Turkey and Greece over immigration. It has affected the cohesion of the EU. It has affected NATO contributions. It is especially, and I think we haven't talked about this, it has made Eastern Europeans far more susceptible to the propaganda of Vladimir Putin who is appealing in a populist sense. If you go to Greece today, you can see that he is the most popular figure there. And his message is a nationalist, populist, Orthodox Christendom message that appeals to people who feel that their own elites in the EU do not listen to what are often legitimate worries about the ability to assimilate and intervene.

And finally, I think it is sort of disingenuous to talk about second generation as if that is not connected with the first generation immigration pattern. If you look at Boston, the Boston Marathon massacre, if you look at Orlando, if you look at San Bernardino, if you look at Fort Hood, we have a reoccurring pattern of second generation Muslims who have been alienated or radicalized and have committed acts of terrorism. So the problem is again with assimilation, integration, intermarriage, and historically throughout society across time and space, if you want to assimilate people, you want to integrate them, you want to intermarry them, and make them part of the body politic, then you don't have problems in the second generation.

Most of the terrorist incidents that are connected with radical Islam in Europe are second generation because of the failure. And we know how we facilitate that process of Americanization and that is by numbers that are manageable, legal, and meritocratic and diverse. We want immigrants from all over the world because having influxes from one particular place or one particular group and not having them live among the population in a dispersed manner makes it much more difficult.

Mr. ROHRABACHER. Dr. Vrbetic.

Ms. VRBETIC. Thank you, Chairman. I would just like to talk a little bit about something that I read about Germany and German schools and their canteens to illustrate the problem that I feel there is with integration. Some of the German schools are dropping pork from menu altogether, and this is because they have a few Muslim kids. Now I am not suggesting that there should be forceful assimilation in the sense of forcing Muslim kids to eat pork. But I don't see why German schools wouldn't offer a variety of choices so that the Muslim kids take their lamb or vegetarians taken their vegetarian meal and those Germans students who want to eat pork, they eat pork. And they all eat this together in a canteen.

But instead, we have a situation there are a few Muslim students, that the German schools drop pork from menu altogether for fear of offending minority. And this is the point that I am trying to make, and this is the issue of toleration.

In liberal democracies, some just push this issue of toleration to the extreme, and when we push it to the extreme, we don't actually encourage toleration as in this case.

By the way, the issue came to the attention of the lawmakers in Schleswig-Holstein, which is one of the German provinces. They wanted to keep pork on the menu.

Going back to this issue, I see the problem between two models. One is liberal multi-culturalism. We try to integrate minorities within this framework. I have exceeded my time. Is that correct?

Mr. ROHRABACHER. No, go ahead. Go ahead.

Ms. VRBETIC. When we try to integrate minorities within this liberal framework. The other is pluralist multi-culturalism, where there are separate minorities, where we set up parallel societies. And the problem with the issue of toleration is that when you push it to the extreme, it becomes politics of indifference. We don't interfere with these communities and we permit, ultimately, some practices that don't stimulate integration and where we end up with both liberal and illiberal elements. I will end here.

Mr. ROHRABACHER. That is a fascinating analysis. Thank you.

Mr. Simcox?

Mr. SIMCOX. The points I would make, first of all, on the kind of the nature of the threat, it is certainly true that in Europe most plots are home grown in nature. There is a little bit more to that in somebody like Salman Abedi, for example, who was the suicide bomber in Manchester last May was second generation Libyan, so it was a home-grown case, but still a refugee element. Yes, most are home grown.

But some of the numbers I have been doing on this between 2004 and 2017, there is 32 plots in Europe, so 8 a year, that were perpetrated by refugees and asylum seekers. So it is not an insignificant number and of course, that includes something like Paris, November 2015, where there was obviously a very large body count.

The other point I would make on the numbers, European experience with integration and assimilation is obviously very different to the U.S. I think the U.S. has always done this much more successfully than we in Europe have, to be honest. So I think of a country like Sweden where I was just there the week before last. They took in 163,000 people in 2015. And obviously, regardless, they consider themselves to be a humanitarian superpower and that they view this as truly, it is like an international obligation.

In terms of what ratio that would be in the U.S., that would be like the U.S. taking in 5.2 million people. It is a very significant number in Sweden. And Sweden, as many in Europe, doesn't really have the experience of making this kind of thing work, like you in the U.S. do. So I would just raise that as one of the potential challenges a lot of Europe countries are going to have to deal with.

Mr. ROHRABACHER. Go for it.

Mr. ALZAYAT. So you know what is interesting is in the European countries with the most refugees, you don't necessarily see correlating fear of refugees. So in Germany, specifically right? They took 1 million Syrians. Not only was Chancellor Merkel at the end of the day elected to a fourth term, but German public opinion of refugees is actually one of the best in Europe. So why is that? Clearly, leadership and the political rhetoric is having something to do with it.

In a place like Hungary and Bulgaria, where you do have far-right parties, who literally were advertising on billboards pretty racist themes against incoming migrants and the threat that will pose to European women specifically, these are societies that have nowhere near the amount of refugees, Muslim refugees, as Germany, yet the public perception and views are quite negative now.

I mean it is a clear indication to me that also leadership, the rhetoric, the policies, play a big role in that. And remember, we are talking about addressing an issue of radicalization potentially.

So my question to everyone is do we think that stereotyping, exclusion, demonization, guilty by association, will lessen the problem of radicalization? Well, address it. And I understand about the fact that maybe there are no more refugees coming right now at the same levels, but the ones that are in Germany, that are in Europe, what is the best way to deal with this situation? They are there right now. It is quite frankly, illegal under international law for those who have been designated as refugees to be refouled to their country of origin without their consent, particularly in places that are experiencing war. So this is now the reality.

So my remarks regarding investing in education, in helping them integrate, in entering the labor force, but also in showing them that tolerance truly applies to them as well is going to have to be key. In terms of percentages, God forbid if 50,000 Muslims in Europe were ISIL followers. We would have a completely different conversation right now. We are talking about tens. That is what we are talking about. That is the number of actual attacks in the tens.

So it is clearly not 1 percent. It is .0001, whether here or abroad. So we have got to assess the problem for what it is and then when you look at that and compare it to the rise in hate crimes, assaults by neo-fascists, and neo-Nazi groups against Jews, against Muslims, and people of color, on both sides of the Atlantic, to me, that is a real worrying trend. And that is what I would really consider as an emerging threat as well.

Mr. ROHRABACHER. Thank you. Can you hear me? Let's just have Dr. Hanson's response.

Mr. HANSON. I think it is a little bit disingenuous because——

Mr. ROHRABACHER. A little louder, Dr. Hanson.

Mr. HANSON. Oh, I am sorry. We are the seeing the largest out migration of Jews since World War II to Israel, and there is a good chance that France within 10 years, if these rates continue, will be—there won't be a sizable Jewish population in France. It is not just terrorism because it is individual attacks on Jewish people who were obviously identified as Jews, Orthodox Jews. There are areas within Paris and I think we have all been to places in Rotterdam and Brussels where if you were to wear a yarmulke, you would be in danger of physical assault. But that is not really the catalyst for that out migration. It is a sense and my colleague here referred to it, there is a sense that the government has lost the confidence and tradition of Western values of tolerance and pluralism.

We are not talking about chauvinism and prejudice and I think Representative Meeks made a good point. What we are talking about is the Western tradition that we all understand and tolerate differences in the periphery of culture, but we unite on democracy and constitutional government and transparency and these core Western values.

Often in inexperience with this number of immigrants or maybe clumsiness or whatever the reason is, European Governments have not been able to address this problem in a liberal sense. They haven't been able to say we welcome you to come in here and it is a two-way street. If you give up some of your identity as all immigrants do and accept the core Western values and that means that if you see people of a different religion or your cultural traditions come in conflict with tolerance and plurality, you have to give that up and we can require that as the host country. But that hasn't been happening in Europe. And that means that we have to deal with it.

The other thing is we would like to lecture Europe and say why don't you look at the United States and see how much a better job we do, but that is not the way nations, there is no international court of good manners. But what happens is we have to make the adjustments of this problem and this problem is going to affect Turkey's membership in NATO in the short term. It is going to affect whether—we can deplore racism all we want. I think we should, but there is a schism growing between Eastern and Western Europe and it is giving Vladimir Putin a lot of opportunities that we don't want. And we have to deal with the world as it is, rather than what we would like it to be.

So I agree with my colleague on the left that we have to reach out, I mean literally the left, not the ideological left.

Mr. ROHRABACHER. See, I can say both of those here.

Mr. HANSON. In a geographical sense, but what I am saying is we have to reach out and try to suggest politely that Europe, without being chauvinistic, might want to learn from the melting pot tradition. It has made us the most diverse country in the world. But in lieu that they might not do that, we have to take security precautions in the United States because I think the EU is seriously facing some existential crises that are going to affect the national security of our alliance.

Mr. ROHRABACHER. We are talking about Western civilization. We are talking about basically the melting pot theories. We are talking about how people—and nationalism. These are forces at play that are part of our analysis of what is going to happen and how to approach this moment in history. And I don't think—this is my opinion that Western civilization has brought more freedom to more people. And the fact that freedom as we know it exists where Western civilization is the dominant force and not the Islamic world which if you look there I don't know any examples of the democratic institutions that we are talking about and we hold dear as Americans. Malaysia? Okay, there is one. Maybe Indonesia, maybe. But when I take a look at those countries that are the most Islamic in terms of actually taking their religion so seriously, there is no freedom in those countries.

In terms of the melting pot, I don't see that you can have a melting pot with people who think that they will not meld in with the notions that other people have a right to worship God as they see fit. Because that is part of the melting pot theory and you do have, I have seen, various opinion polls taken in London, I believe it was, that suggested that those people, those Islamic people in London, well, of all the people who were saying no, people do not have the right to worship God as they see fit, if it is different than my faith, almost all of them are Muslims and almost none of them are Christians, saying no, if someone disagrees with me and my faith, they don't have a right to practice it. Almost all the ones who say well, and I don't believe—Mr. Meeks, just to be fair about it, I don't think the interpretation, I mean I know that we have been told that we have to assume that Islam is a faith of peace and it means—but Islam to some interpretations and correct me, you probably know more about this than I do, that Islam means submission. The more accurate interpretation is submission, not peace. And for those who don't submit, it is anything but peace. Is that right?

Mr. ALZAYAT. Islam comes from the word salaam and that is peace.

Mr. ROHRABACHER. Okay. All right.

Mr. ALZAYAT. In fact, you know, the greeting of Muslims is peace be upon you. It is not you shall submit to me.

Mr. ROHRABACHER. Okay, well, I am sure—salaam alaikum. Okay, well, I will have to admit that I just don't see any countries in the world right now cutting the heads off where Christians are cutting the heads off Muslims, but I have seen the opposite. And all I am saying here is you don't—obviously, you cannot put all Muslims in one category, but you can realize that when you see things happening, if there is a significant more of Muslims doing something that is something you don't want to happen in your society, like refuse to recognize somebody else's right to worship God as they see fit, well, then you should be aware of that. That should be something and also in second generation type of things where we are talking about, yes, we have had people in our own country and our own culture, Dr. Hanson, we have had our own people shooting kids up at schools that have nothing to do with Islam, but in terms of the Muslim population, the number of Muslims here and the number of actual situations where second generation Muslims have gone crazy, it is very demonstrable and I don't know another case like in San Bernardino where you had that.

Dr. Hanson, basically, do you have second generation Christians coming here and doing that? I don't remember one case of that happening, where someone who has immigrated here from another country and is a Christian or as a Buddhist or some other religion, I don't know one case where the second generation Buddhist or second generation Christian went out and committed these mass murders. Maybe you can enlighten me.

Mr. ALZAYAT. You have fourth, fifth, sixth generation Christians are committing it. So that is actually even more worrying.

Mr. ROHRABACHER. Well, that is skipping the question. Do you have—that is getting around the question.

Mr. ALZAYAT. So when we have, for example, you know, well, by the way when we say a white Christian, no one knows how religious these people are or whether they are true believers. In fact, I doubt their faith if they were true Christians, they wouldn't do this. But that aside, you have statistically speaking far more violence by white Christian males in this country, statistically speaking, than any other group. Excuse me, I didn't interrupt you. And so what you have is right now amplification of a particular problem. It is a real problem. Terrorism in the name of Islam is a real problem and needs to be dealt with. We are not ignoring it, but what we are saying is that are we being fair to the religion and its adherence and people, the overwhelming majority of people who condemn it and are looking for real ways to address it.

As Americans, we have to be honest about the numbers in this country in terms of the actual attacks that have happened, by which groups, and address them accordingly. From Oklahoma City to the mail bombs in Austin, just a few weeks ago, to Charlottesville, clearly other people—the Waffle House just a few days, to the horrible school shootings——

Mr. ROHRABACHER. And which ones of those were motivated by religion?

Mr. ALZAYAT. They were all Christian.

Mr. ROHRABACHER. It wasn't based on anybody's religion.

Mr. ALZAYAT. How do we know that the Muslims did it because of religion and not just because they were horrible people or they had mental illness?

Mr. ROHRABACHER. I think that there has been indication.

Dr. Hanson, do you want to say something and then we will let Mr. Meeks go.

Mr. HANSON. We don't know how disingenuous anybody is who commits a crime, but we can only go on the pretext of what they say and it is a matter of fact that violent incidents that have a political agenda, the perpetrators have identified themselves as self-appointed representatives of Islam and we don't have corresponding numbers. In a country that is about 80 percent self-identified as Christian, we don't have corresponding numbers of people who commit violence against people who are not Christian because of a Christian identity. That is just a fact.

So to say——

Mr. ALZAYAT. Oklahoma City is a political bombing.

Mr. HANSON. No, it was not a Christian bombing.

Mr. ALZAYAT. Political terrorist bombing, in fact.

Mr. HANSON. It was not a Christian bombing against non-Christians. When we go outside this building, most—you asked me not to interrupt. I would request the same courtesy from you. When we go outside this building, most of the people today who commit traffic accidents, most of the people who jaywalk, will be Christian. So that citation means almost nothing in a predominantly Christian country.

What we are talking about is politically-motivated violence by people who self-identify, even if they misuse the religion, with a particular religion against people they feel are enemies of that religion.

Mr. ALZAYAT. Well, that is Srebrenica.

Mr. HANSON. I am talking about inside the United States.

Mr. MEEKS. Even in the United States, if I can——

Mr. ALZAYAT. In Srebrenica, there were 10,000 Muslims who were butchered by fundamentalist Christians in Serbia in the name of religion.

Mr. ROHRABACHER. That is absolutely correct.

Mr. MEEKS. But even in the United States——

Mr. ROHRABACHER. Mr. Meeks.

Mr. MEEKS. Let me just say this because I have to go.

Mr. ROHRABACHER. Mr. Meeks has the floor.

Mr. MEEKS. Because even in the United States, the Ku Klux Klan identify themselves as Christians and they believe in the Bible, slavery, the slave masters said that they could enslave people in Christianity in the name of Christ. They believe that is what they did.

You talk to white nationalists today, they will tell you they are acting in the same manner as the Bible calls for, that slavery is okay because it is in the Bible. I have met and talked to them. When I was raised, my parents were raised in the South and within my lifetime, a lot of what they have done was in the name of Christianity and justified what they did by being Christians.

Now in response also though to this whole—I think Mr. Rohrabacher, what you just indicated in regards to this nation or that nation, you know, they don't have Western principles, etcetera, but let me just say this, even democracy, because for me and my father, didn't have democracy in America. So democracy that is something that is out there for most—I can recall being in South Carolina and my grandfather, my father, my mother, not being able to vote. I can recall being told I had to get underneath the bed as my grandfather got on the porch with a shotgun because folks who went to church on Sunday morning were now coming to get the so-called N people. This is in my lifetime that I have witnessed.

And then you also talk about democracies in many of these other places, these places were places that were colonized by the West and brutal dictators were put in place to keep them in order. And this is less than 50, 60 years ago. They were colonies of Western democracies. And there were certain things that was done to put—and so some of what you talk was put into place to keep them in certain controls, whether you talk about the Middle East, whether you talk about Asia, whether you talk about Africa, all of these places were colonized by Western so-called democracies.

If you look at our country, 25, 30 years, 40 years, 50 years, this was the wild wild West, all kind of craziness was going on. And so now we are 240 years later and there are still problems. So to go after some other country who has a new democracy, basically an infant, and try to compare it to the democracy of the United States, which still needs a lot of work, to me is like comparing apples to oranges.

And what we need to be doing in one sense, people are—one of the things we have in common is our—we are all human. No matter what our race or our religion, we are human. And so we should be focusing on the human problems and people leave from one area to another because there is a human problem that exists. And so they all—that is why I used my family's experience as an example of people trying to go someplace else. My parents would never have left South Carolina if they had an opportunity there. Never would have left. I might have been a member from South Carolina instead of New York. But they left because they needed an opportunity. They went to a place that they thought they could have a better life for their family.

So it is the same thing when you have a lot of individuals—they are not leaving Syria just because they want to leave Syria. They are leaving Syria for a reason. In fact, that was one of my questions. You know, sometimes it is easy for us to say go bomb. But there is consequences, because we don't look at the human lives that are affected by the bombing. The women and children and men who are innocent, who just want to—they leave because—they are not leaving because of some kind of religion or something, their homes are bombed. There is no place for them to go or to eat. They are starving. So if the bombing didn't take place, we wouldn't have had some of this situation.

I mean one of the questions I had, you know, I was going to ask Mr. Alzayat, what role did the Russia bombing of Aleppo have in forcing migration of hundreds of thousands of people to Turkey? Did it play a role in that?

Mr. ALZAYAT. It played a direct role. I was the outreach coordinator for Ambassador Robert Ford with the Syrian communities, really, activists, NGOs, and opposition members as well and our allies in Europe, particularly who were working on this. And as soon as the Russians started bombing, they were bombing—they were not bombing the terrorists. They were not bombing ISIL. They were not bombing al-Qaeda. They were bombing civilians who were opposed to Bashar al-Assad and what we term the Free Syria Army groups with all of their imperfections.

And there was a direct correlation, so that when they were bombing Aleppo, they were bombing the areas around Homs in northern Syria and other areas. You saw massive movement. Hundreds of thousands of people pushing into Turkey. At the time, Turkey had almost close to 2 million people by then. And so they released the valves to let people go into Europe and that is the European migration crisis.

In a sense, it was weaponized against Europe. That is what happened.

Mr. HANSON. If I could make a concluding remark. I think the sins of mankind are what Representative Meeks enunciated. Every country has had that history, Western or non-Western.

What is unique about the West it has a tradition of self-critique, self-examination to rectify. The FBI destroyed the Klan in the 1960s, and so even Klanwatch and Southern Poverty Law Center now have branched out into other areas of hatred because the country healed itself. It had a debate. It found the right chords.

And that process of self-introspection is why people from the Muslim world and the non-West come to the West. And so it is the height of irony that people are coming to the West for freedom and for diversity and self-critique and then when they arrive the host has lost the confidence of its own traditions to say to them, you came here for a reason. It wasn't just economic opportunity, you wanted respect as an individual, so all we require of you is that you adopt the customs and the traditions that are not perfect, but we don't have to be perfect to be good. And we have a unique tradition of self-critique and change. That is all, I think, we are trying to suggest is that Europe's problem is that for some reason we don't have time to get into it, it has not been able to tell its immigrant population that you have to assimilate. Not change your food, your religion, your fashion, your cultural pride and traditions, but to accept a body of tolerance for everybody who believes, or looks, or acts in a different way. And I know that minority of immigrants may be small, but the pool is large enough that a very small minority can be very volatile. In a country like Europe, it doesn't have our experience with assimilation and immigration.

Mr. SIMCOX. I will only take 2 minutes. I would just make the point, reiterate the point really that what applies to the U.S., doesn't necessarily apply to Europe. You have had—the melting pot in the U.S. has never worked in Europe in the same way. And so I would just encourage us not to view these two situations as entirely analogous.

Of course, the situation in Syria, there is no doubt it is horrendous, horrendous what has happened in Syria. And there has to be a response from the international community. It is an irresponsible response, I believe, to say that Europe should be the home of millions of people, that it didn't have the chance to vet and somehow if Europe doesn't do that, it is not living up to its international commitment through somehow being unreasonable. This is a very, very difficult situation for Europe. Integration has been failing in Europe for some time. So adding millions more people into the mix is—obviously, the humanitarian impulse is there, but we can't wish away the problems that that sort of thing can create. So I would just encourage us all to be at least aware of that and not necessarily think of this as being just like the U.S. experience.

Ms. VRBETIC. Thank you, Mr. Chairman. I would agree that the terror acts are committed by a small group of people, but what we are really talking about is what is the fact. And the fact on European societies and European politics has been tremendous. And this is what we worry about. How Europe is changing politically and the divisions within Europe and this is not good for Europe. Russia is certainly going to exploit us.

And also, I wanted to say what I started talking, I think Dr. Hanson took it over, and this is really that the European societies need to have more confidence and make demands on the minorities, clear demands for integration, not for assimilation, but for integration and for respect of the liberal traditions and I think that would be also a big contribution to where it is having more cohesive societies in Europe and toward eliminating some of the problems we are talking about here.

Mr. ALZAYAT. Clearly, this is a difficult issue. These societies are dealing with really frustrating dynamics. We are all humans and we hate change and we also don't like insecurity and Europeans have had to deal with that.

The question is what is the best way to deal with it? And my argument is really based on our own experience here in the United States. Integration cannot be forced. When you try to force it, you get some of that toxicity. People have to want to be French, to want to be German, and most of them do. That is what I am trying to point out. Actually, most of them do. Ninety-four percent said they felt connected to the country. Seventy-five percent are intermingling with other religions. So I don't know about that whole statement that they are not doing that. They are. These are the facts.

And how we approach the subject is extremely important because half of the Muslim population in Europe is under the age of 30. Forcing them will not work. It will not work. Engaging them, investing and educating them and removing institutional, discriminatory barriers that society, particularly, the educational system, encouraging them to be public servants, civil servants, diplomats, police officers, soldiers of their new country, is one of the best ways. Or let them do whatever they want. They don't have to be held to any higher standard, but it is that freedom to express their religiosity, as long as all of them support the tenets and the principles of the Western European order, freedom, respect of the individual, absolutely. It is what every human being irrespective of their religion deserves.

And so I thank you for the opportunity today. You know, we are not going to resolve this today, but anything that will help people abroad and make us safe here, we are game for it, so thank you for inviting us.

Mr. ROHRABACHER. Well, I thank all of you and I will reserve the final statement for the chairman, but I did appreciate the lively discussions we had. Mr. Meeks and I are very close friends, so don't think that because he gets excited and I may get excited at times that we are anything but very good friends and respect each other's opinion.

With that said, I think that as I say, the issues that are at the heart of this discussion has something to do also with how you value Western civilization and whether or not you believe that the influx coming in from the Middle East that is going into Europe today will in some way diminish Western civilization's influence on humanity. And I have to say that I think, I believe, that that is what is happening. No matter what you can say about vetting and what may be the goals, etcetera, that in the end what we will see is a diminishing of the influence on humankind of what we call Western civilization.

I think that to a degree that you have got nationalism at play in Eastern Europe and elsewhere in Europe, it is that these people and like the Pole, for example, who are instrumental in defeating the Muslim advance into Europe and stopped them at Vienna, that is something they are very proud of there. And I can see where that is part of their framework, they say. We will defend Western civilization. And that is their nationalism, it is an expression of their nationals. And it is probably true with the Hungarians. And it is probably true with these other countries that we are talking about. Whether or not this influx from, in a very trying situation, where people desperately are trying to escape a war zone, whether or not that is something that is more important to take care of them than in other people's view than to preserve Western civilization only if that does not in some way threaten it. But I believe a lot of people do believe it is a threat and do believe that there will be major impact on their way of life. And I think that that is not an irrational thing, although I think you have made a really good case today. Seriously, you have done a really good job of presenting thoughtful challenges to what I just said which is fine. That is fine.

And I will say that I do not think nationalism is a bad thing, but it can be a bad thing. Obviously, Adolph Hitler was a bad guy, but to the degree of nationalism is used as it is in the United States to say we are Americans and we believe in this, we believe in freedom, that is different. It is a different thing.

And if we have people who, it is not racial, but people who come in that have another faith from what Western civilization has done for the United States which has been predominantly a Christian, Western-oriented population from early on. Yes, we stole it from the Indians. I admit it. Okay. There is no doubt about that. But by and large, the people who came to the United States were Christians, who came here seeking freedom, but they all weren't required, for example, where there were a lot of Catholics around, they didn't outlaw the eating the meat on Friday.

When I was younger, I remember that the Catholics didn't eat meat on Friday. Now I understand that has been changed now, but I remember that very well. At no time did Catholics advocate that in their town that they not sell or eat meat on Friday. There is something there that indicates that when you are taking a poll and again, I wish I had a poll here to show you, that indicates that those people who adamantly believe in Islam are willing to say that other people should not have that right to make their choices, I think that is why you saw these beheadings, what happened in the Middle East.

In terms of the number of people who are suffering there, a lot of it, you are right. It has nothing to do with Islam. It has everything to do with power grabs by power mongers.

I will have to say this about Assad. I think he is no better or worse than the other dictators there, whether they call themselves kings or royal families or just the power brokers or whatever title they have given themselves, when someone challenges them, they slaughter the opposition. And that is one thing that I think is not acceptable. But it also may mean that we should not necessarily be jumping into that whole can of worms and thinking that we are going to start giving the orders and telling people how to solve the problem because I think it is going to be a long time before that problem is solved.

And with that said, I am sorry for going on. I just want to thank all of you. I think there's been—we didn't come to any conclusion, but I think this has been very provocative today. So thank you and this hearing is adjourned.

[Whereupon, at 3:56 p.m., the subcommittee was adjourned.]

APPENDIX

SUBCOMMITTEE HEARING NOTICE
COMMITTEE ON FOREIGN AFFAIRS
U.S. HOUSE OF REPRESENTATIVES
WASHINGTON, DC 20515-6128

Subcommittee on Europe, Eurasia, and Emerging Threats
Dana Rohrabacher (R-CA), Chairman

April 24, 2018

TO: MEMBERS OF THE COMMITTEE ON FOREIGN AFFAIRS

You are respectfully requested to attend an OPEN hearing of the Committee on Foreign Affairs to be held by the Subcommittee on Europe, Eurasia, and Emerging Threats in Room 2200 of the Rayburn House Office Building (and available live on the Committee website at http://www.ForeignAffairs.house.gov):

DATE: Thursday, April 26, 2018

TIME: 1:00 p.m.

SUBJECT: Mass Migration in Europe: Assimilation, Integration, and Security

WITNESSES: Victor Davis Hanson, Ph.D.
Martin and Illie Anderson Senior Fellow
Hoover Institution
Stanford University

Marta Vrbetic, Ph.D.
Global Fellow
Global Europe Program
Woodrow Wilson International Center for Scholars

Mr. Robin Simcox
Margaret Thatcher Fellow
Margaret Thatcher Center for Freedom
Davis Institute for National Security and Foreign Policy
The Heritage Foundation

Mr. Wa'el Alzayat
Chief Executive Officer
Emgage

By Direction of the Chairman

The Committee on Foreign Affairs seeks to make its facilities accessible to persons with disabilities. If you are in need of special accommodations, please call 202/225-5021 at least four business days in advance of the event, whenever practicable. Questions with regard to special accommodations in general (including availability of Committee materials in alternative formats and assistive listening devices) may be directed to the Committee.

COMMITTEE ON FOREIGN AFFAIRS

MINUTES OF SUBCOMMITTEE ON ___*Europe, Eurasia, and Emerging Threats*___ HEARING

Day___*Thursday*___ Date___*April 26, 2018*___ Room___*2200 RHOB*___

Starting Time ___*1:00 pm*___ Ending Time ___*3:56 pm*___

Recesses | *1* | (*2:12 pm* to *3:12 pm*) (___to___) (___to___) (___to___) (___to___) (___to___)

Presiding Member(s)

Rep. Rohrabacher

Check all of the following that apply:

Open Session ☑
Executive (closed) Session ☐
Televised ☐

Electronically Recorded (taped) ☑
Stenographic Record ☑

TITLE OF HEARING:

Mass Migration in Europe: Assimilation, Integration, and Security

SUBCOMMITTEE MEMBERS PRESENT:

Rep. Meeks, Rep. Cicilline, Rep. Kelly

NON-SUBCOMMITTEE MEMBERS PRESENT: *(Mark with an * if they are not members of full committee.)*

N/A

HEARING WITNESSES: Same as meeting notice attached? Yes ☑ No ☐
(If "no", please list below and include title, agency, department, or organization.)

STATEMENTS FOR THE RECORD: *(List any statements submitted for the record.)*

Attached

TIME SCHEDULED TO RECONVENE ___
or
TIME ADJOURNED ___*3:56 pm*___

Subcommittee/Staff Associate

The EU response to the migration crisis

Background material

Has the European migration crisis been resolved?

Europe as a continent hosts the second largest population of international migrants globally (78 M people).[1] Besides being a continent of traditional immigration, it has been witnessing a massive influx of irregular migrants since 2015. According to Eurostat figures, a total number of 3.3 million asylum applications were submitted in the EU-28 between 2015 and 2017.[2] This 3-year period means a historical peak in this regard for the continent.

Figure 1: Total number of asylum applications submitted in the EU-28

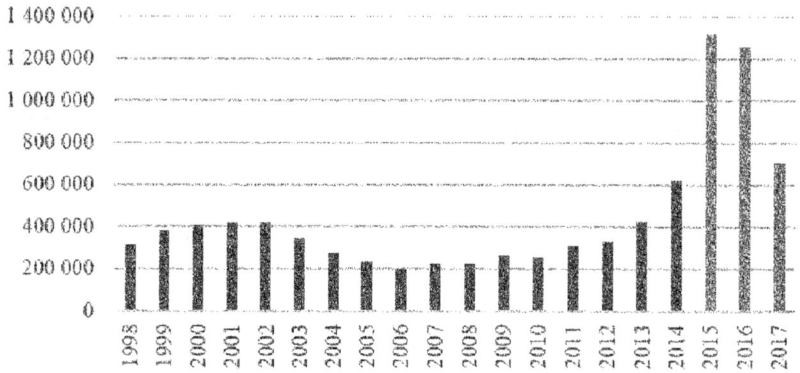

Source: Eurostat (Downloaded on: 23/04/2018)

Germany has been the top receiving country in the EU since 2015, accepting nearly half (1.44 M) of the total applications alone. These data potentially include some duplications (i.e. there are thousand of asylum applicants who have submitted multiple applications in more than one EU Member State). Nevertheless, the number of illegal border-crossings (IGC, statistics collected and released by FRONTEX) also show significantly higher numbers than ever before. The three main entry points into the territory of the EU saw the following IGC number in the already mentioned period: Eastern Mediterranean route (Greece-Turkey) 1.1 million, Central Mediterranean route (Libya-Italy) 450 thousand, and the Western Mediterranean route (predominantly Morocco-Spain) 40 thousand.[3] It is important to note that the Western Balkan route was greatly affected by the migration crisis: in 2015, it witnessed more than 764 thousand IGCs. All in all, the effective number of those arriving to the EU must have exceeded 1.5 million since 2015.

As for the citizenship of applicants, the people concerned show a great level of concentration: Afghans (416 thousand), Iraqis (307 thousand) and Syrians (813 thousand) altogether represent

---

[1] https://publications.iom.int/system/files/pdf/wmr_2018_update_international_migrants_a4.pdf (Downloaded on: 23/04/2018).

[2] http://ec.europa.eu/eurostat/data/database (Downloaded on: 23/04/2018)

[3] https://frontex.europa.eu/ (Downloaded on: 23/04/2018)

more than 1.5 million applications. The socio-demographic profile of asylum applicants looks as follows: 69% of them are aged between 18–64 years, and the majority are males (also 69%).

Due to the crisis management measures adopted and implemented from 2016, the volume of effective arrivals has moderated since the peak of the crisis. It is important to highlight two set of measures: first, the gradual closing of borders on the Western Balkan until spring of 2016 (starting with Hungary in autumn 2015). Second, the EU-Turkey Pact entered into force in March 2016, which has proved to be an efficient tool in mitigating the uncontrolled influx through the Greek-Turkish border ever since.

Figure 2: Number of arrivals from Turkey to the Greek islands in 2016

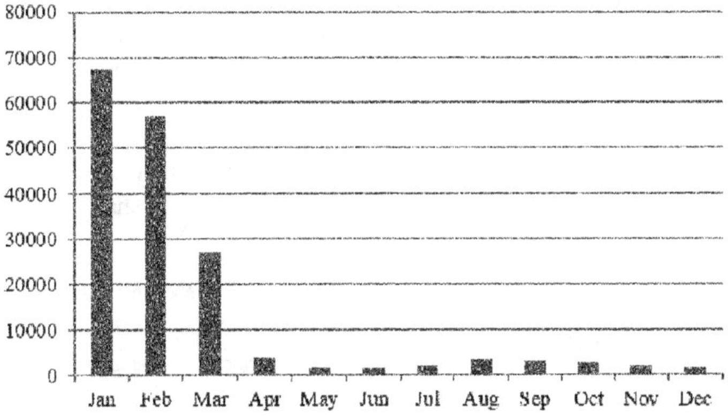

Source: Frontex (Downloaded on: 23/04/2018)

Despite the improvements indicated above, the intensity of the influx to Europe seems to remain high. In fact, what has been happening since spring 2016 is the adaptation of migrants and human smugglers to the changed situation. Following the entry into force of the EU-Turkey migration pact and the efficient addressing of the Balkan situation, the Central Mediterranean route (that is from Libya to Italy) has be re-discovered by migrants and smugglers, exploiting the chaotic situation of the North African country. As a result, Italy had to face an unprecedented migratory pressure until mid-2017, when the Italian government strengthened its cooperation with the internationally recognised Libyan government and decided to take steps against the controversially operating NGOs active in search and rescue operations in the Mediterranean. The outcome was convincing: Italy could ease the pressure, a development also clearly visible from FRONTEX data. One should note that Italy shows a great example of how migratory challenges can be efficiently addressed in the short run, but this is something a Member State on its own could achieve, without meaningful help or support from Brussels.

The EU-Turkey pact proved to be a very useful instrument in securing Greece's EU external borders. However, it is important to remember that the EU was completely paralysed in 2015, meaning that it was even unable to secure its external borders. As a key element of managing the crisis, the controversial decision on relocation quotas was adopted by the European Council in autumn 2015, which has proved to be a clear failure. At the same time, the Member States who positioned themselves against this measure (in the first place, Hungary) have been subject to heavy criticism from both Brussels and Western EU Member States, claiming the lack of solidarity from the side of these countries. Later, this position has become shared by several

Member States, in particular the Visegrad countries (including the Czech Republic, Poland and Slovakia in addition to Hungary).

In the meantime, when the EU seems to be captured in the illusion of making the quota system working and accepted, the pressure on the EU does not seem to ease. The fact that migrants and smugglers keep seeking alternative routes to Europe, as well as the migration potential in the Middle East and in particular in North and the Sub-Saharan Africa remain a challenge for the EU. In Turkey alone, there are more than 3.5 million Syrian refugees residing at the moment, and a part of them definitely would be happy to leave for the EU whenever possible. But the migration story is far not about Syrians any more: Afghans, Iranians and Iraqis often face much more hopeless situation in the place where they reside, and we see greater and greater number of migrants leaving North African countries like Morocco, Algeria or Tunisia (leaving for Spain). The Sub-Saharan Africa promises the greatest potential for further irregular migration to Europe in the decades to come: in Libya alone, an estimated number of 0.7–1 million migrants (predominantly arriving from the mentioned region) were waiting in late 2017 to leave for Europe.[4] As for the desire to migrate, Sub-Sharan Africa presents a worrisome picture: between 2013 and 2016, some 31% of the adult population of the region expressed that they would move to another country if possible.[5] We see extreme high shares in certain countries (see *Table 1*).

Table 1: Share of adult population planning to migrate in selected African countries (%)

SIERRA LEONE	**62**
LIBERIA	**54**
CONGO	**50**
GHANA	**45**
NIGERIA	**43**
SUDAN	**37**
GUINEA	**36**

Source: Gallup (Downloaded on: 23/04/2018)

The Pew Research Center found similarly high desire and potential to migrate in Sub-Saharan countries in its respective survey.[6]

The push factors responsible for the large outflow of people – in the first place, those of economic nature – need to be addressed by the EU to reduce irregular immigration in the long run, an objective of strategic importance. In the meantime, securing external borders and deporting those not eligible for any type of international protection is crucial to regain control of the European migration processes. Europe is still too far from this.

Are those arriving to Europe actual refugees or economic migrants?

From 2016, a shift has occurred due to the developments briefly outlined above. The new arrivals to the EU after 2015 and 2016 became more diverse regarding the nationality background: the dominance of those from the Middle East reduced, and North and Sub-Saharan

---

[4] https://www.iom.int/news/un-migration-agency-moves-relieve-plight-migrants-trapped-libya-backing-au-eu-plan (Downloaded on: 23/04/2018)

[5] news.gallup.com/poll/211883/number-potential-migrants-worldwide-tops-700-million.aspx?g_source=World&g_medium=newsfeed&g_campaign=tiles (Downloaded on: 23/04/2018)

[6] 5. http://www.pewglobal.org/2018/03/22/at-least-a-million-sub-saharan-africans-moved-to-europe-since-2010/ (Downloaded on: 23/04/2018)

African migrants gained greater share. According to a study ordered by the UNHCR last year, 7 out of 10 people leaving Libya for Europe qualify as economic migrant.[7]

The share of actual refugees (i.e. those who subsequently proved to be eligible for and were finally granted some type of international protection) has been relatively low since 2015. The aggregate recognition rate[8] of non-EU citizens in the EU-28 was 15% in 2015, 17% in 2016 and 37% in 2017, respectively.[9] If we have a look at the nationality, data for 2017 reveal that Syrians (94%) and Eritreans (84%) were the most likely to be granted a protection status, followed by Afghans (54%), Iranians (50%) and Iraqis (43%). Some selected African nationals – representing an increasing share among irregular arrivals – produce much worse figures: asylum applicants from Guinea and Nigeria had an 18% recognition rate last year, meaning that more than 10,000 persons from these two countries were refused to lawfully stay in the respective Member State. The recognition rates reinforce the statement that the majority of those who have arrived to the continent since 2016 are not eligible for international protection, and rather qualify as economic migrants.

What are the consequences of the large-scale influx to Europe?

Germany provides a good proxy when examining the consequences of large-scale migration to Europe (see the outstanding number of asylum applications submitted in the country). This type of migration is accompanied by a wide range of risks: cultural-religious, security, economic, political etc. Germany is in a special situation, since the number of people with immigration background living in the country reached 18.6 million by the end of 2016, some 22.5% of its total population. Naturally, mass migration has further accelerated this process. The majority of those who have recently arrived to the country are male, aged between 18 and 34, and follow the teachings of Islam.

According to a survey cited in a study prepared for the European Parliament, 35% of asylum applicants in Germany did not ever participated in any type of formal education before, 41% was educated in primary or maximum secondary education institutions, and only one-fifth of them took part in higher education.[10] Similarly, the foreign language knowledge is also very poor of these people, and the majority of them lacks any work experience from the past. Accordingly, it is not surprising that German companies are not willing to employ refugees or immigrants. As a result, the unemployment rate of recent refugees peaked above 50% in mid-2017, while their employment rate stood at only 20% in Germany.[11] These are the facts despite the efforts of the German government to integrate these people on the labour market: in 2016, it spent a total amount of EUR 21.7 billion on managing the migration crisis, including large amounts for integration measures. According to the former German finance minister's expectations, Germany would possibly spend a total amount of EUR 94 billion on crisis management until 2020. Even in the medium run it seems hardly probable to see any benefits in economic terms for the receiving countries (here, Germany).

Beyond the clear-cut relationship between the hike in terrorist threat throughout Western Europe and uncontrolled, irregular mass migration to the continent (see the tragic events in

---

[7] http://www.unhcr.org/595a02b44.pdf (Downloaded on: 23/04/2018)
[8] Recognition rate = total positive decisions / total decisions (final and binding decisions)
[9] Eurostat (Downloaded on: 23/04/2018)
[10] http://www.europarl.europa.eu/RegData/etudes/STUD/2018/614200/IPOL_STU(2018)614200_EN.pdf (Downloaded on: 23/04/2018)
[11] Ibid.

Paris in November 2015), the public security situation generally deteriorated in the largest receiving countries. In Germany, according to available crime figures, the total number of reported criminal offences reached 6.4 million, a 0.7% increase compared to 2015.[12] In the background, the number of suspects with German citizenship decreased in recent years, that of those without German citizenship grew by 40% in two decades. In 2016, the share of suspects with foreign citizenship represented 40% regarding all criminal offences committed in the country. This is a rather negative development, since foreign citizens make up only 10.5% of Germany's population. Non-German suspects are heavily overrepresented in each crime category. The federal crime statistics distinguishes a separate category of "immigrants", which includes, among others, asylum applicants. The share of individuals belonging to the latter category within all suspects increased from 5.7% in 2015 to 8.6% in 2016. The seriousness of the problem becomes more pronounced if we add that "immigrants" make up only 2% of Germany's population.

What policy measures did Hungary take to address irregular migration?

In 2015 Hungary's main goal was to cut back irregular migration, to gain back control over its southern border, to ensure effective border protection and to establish a new legal framework for the asylum procedure. In order to achieve these, a number of new legislation and decrees were adopted in July and September 2015, as well as consistently implemented thereafter. These included the set-up of a border fence at the southern border of Hungary with Serbia and Croatia. Along with this, a new "border procedure" was introduced prescribing the mandatory submission of asylum applications in the so-called "transit zones", which are in compliance with EU legislation. In addition, the "safe third country" concept was introduced, including Greece, Macedonia and Serbia as countries to where rejected asylum applicants can be sent back without exposing them to any threat. Simultaneously, the illegal crossing of the border fence became subject to the Criminal Code as criminal offence, punishable by actual or suspended imprisonment up to 10 years.

In 2016 the government adopted further amendment to the Asylum Act (effective from July 2016) in order to improve the efficiency of the border fence and transit zones, as well as to establish the legal grounds for more effective enforcement of legislation adopted and implemented in mid-2015. The so-called "8 km rule" as new regulation aimed to force migrants who arrived to the country irregularly to enter the transit zones from the Serbian side of the border so they can submit their applications lawfully. We could say that the amendment aimed to supplement the previously adopted legislation since the authorities were thus provided a legal tool to deal with those who were actually not caught damaging and crossing the border fence illegally but entered the country by circumventing the entry into one of the "transit zones".

---

[12] https://www.bka.de/DE/AktuelleInformationen/StatistikenLagebilder/PolizeilicheKriminalstatistik/PKS2016/pks2016_node.html (Downloaded on: 23/04/2018)

Figure 3: Number of asylum applications submitted in Hungary

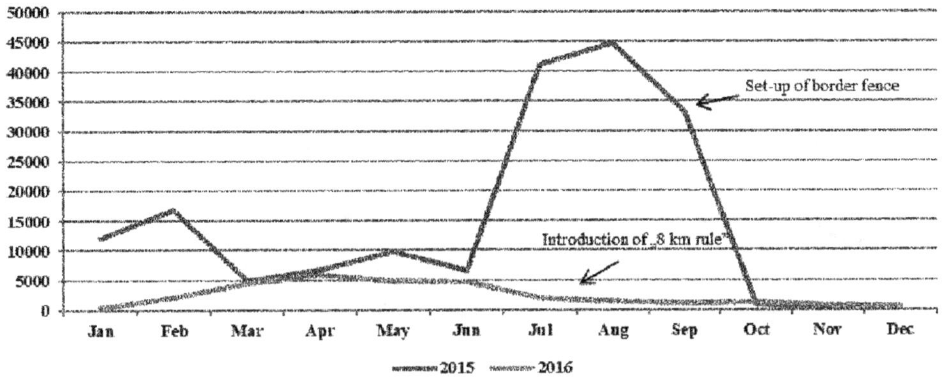

Source: Eurostat (Downloaded on: 23/04/2018)

On 7 March 2017 the Hungarian Parliament approved the legislation on restricting the procedure conducted at the border control area. According to the new rules, the free movement of the rejected asylum applicants and of those without a final decision became restricted, meaning that a specific place (the "transit zone") was appointed where the concerned persons have to wait during the period of processing their application. (Previously, asylum applicants eligible to submit application were transported to open reception centres until the end of the procedure, provided with the possibility of free movement – which practice significantly contributed to the losing sight of these persons.) This also ensures that the asylum procedure is conducted at the border. Besides, the "8 km rule" was also expanded, enabling the escort of migrants back to the border from any part of Hungary. Pursuant to the adopted rules, the asylum applicant may only leave the "transit zone" with the permission of the authority, otherwise they may be imprisoned. However, asylum applicants are free to leave for Serbia at any phase of the procedure.

The results of Hungary's measures taken in the field of combatting irregular migration are convincing: the number of illegal border-crossings was reduced to levels near zero.

What do Europeans think about the migration crisis and its management?

According to the results of various public opinion polls, most Europeans are concerned by two closely related topics: immigration and terrorism.[13] The Eurobarometer provides public opinion data for the EU-28, surveyed in every six months. Since the outbreak of the migration crisis, concerns regarding the economic and unemployment situation have moderated, and the mentioned two issues have taken the very first place among European citizens.

---

[13]

http://ec.europa.eu/commfrontoffice/publicopinion/index.cfm/Survey/getSurveyDetail/instruments/STANDARD/surveyKy/2142 (Downloaded on: 23/04/2018)

Figure 4: „What do you think are the two most important issues facing the EU at the moment? (%, two answers maximum)

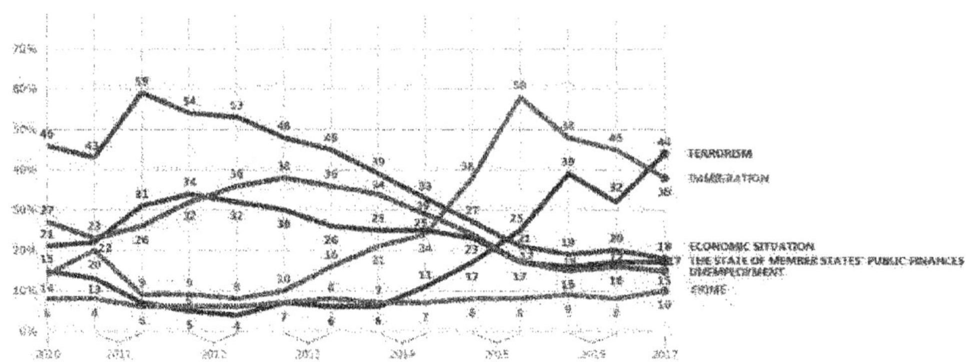

Source: Eurobarometer, Spring 2017 (Downloaded on: 23/04/2018)

Similarly, the Project28 survey conducted by Századvég Foundation in the EU-28 found that illegal immigration means a concern to the overwhelming majority of the Europeans.[14]

Figure 5: „ How serious a problem do you believe it is that illegal immigrants are coming into your country?" (EU-28)

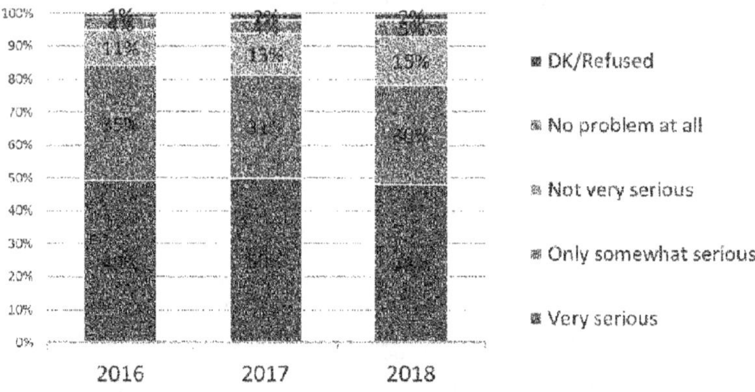

Source: Project28, poll 2018

In line with the description above on the nature of the European migration crisis, the majority believes that most people coming to the EU qualify as economic migrants instead of people in need of humanitarian help.

---

[14] http://project28.eu/ (Downloaded on: 23/04/2018)

Figure 6: „Which of the following statement describes the current situation better?" (EU-28)

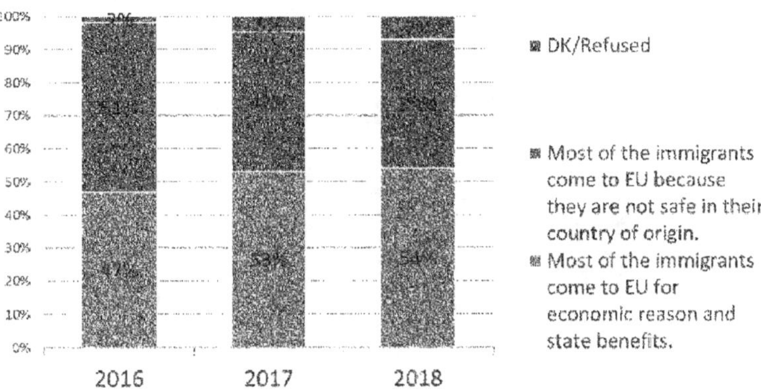

Source: Project28, poll 2018

EU citizens also find relationship between the deterioration of public security, increasing threat of terrorism and the mass influx of people.

Figure 7: "The influx of immigrants to your country will increase the threat of terrorism" (EU-28)

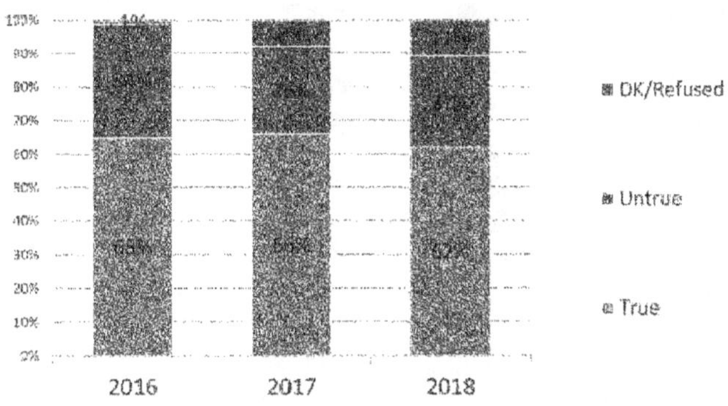

Source: Project28, poll 2018

In the meantime, the Europeans are not satisfied with the efforts of Brussels to address the challenges of mass migration. Instead, slight majority of the respondents said that East-Central European countries have performed better in managing the crisis situation (securing external borders). Also in this regard, EU citizens are greatly divided in their opinions about the so-called "quota system".

Figure 8: "Who do you believe has handled the immigration crisis better?"

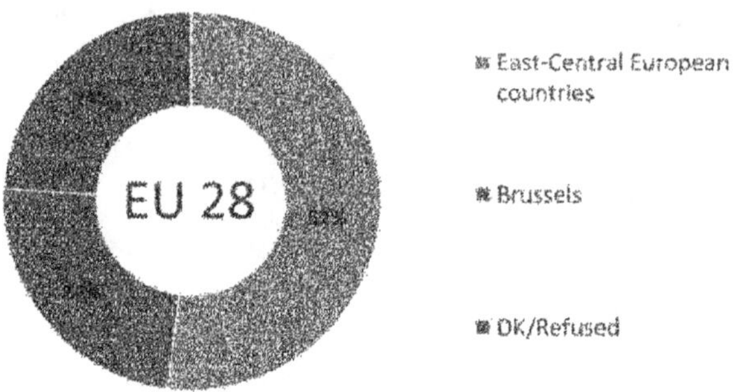

Source: Project28, poll 2018

Figure 9: "The European Union quota plan to distribute recent immigrants throughout Europe" (EU-28)

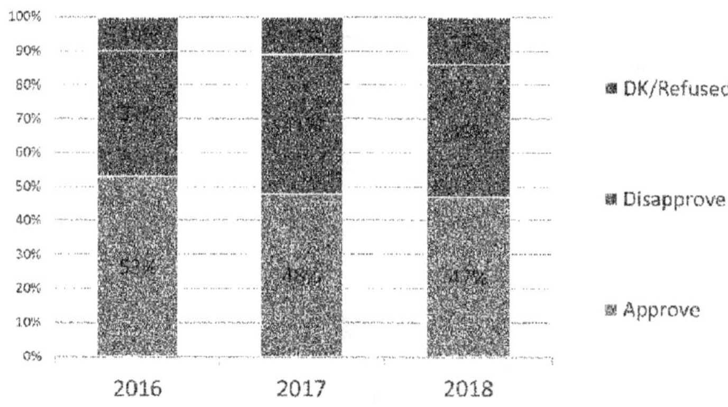

Source: Project28, poll 2018

The Ambassador of Hungary

The Honorable Dana Rohrabacher
U.S. House of Representatives
Washington, D.C.

Washington, D.C., April 24, 2018

Dear Congressman Rohrabacher

I welcome the timely debate of the Subcommittee for Europe, Eurasia and Emerging Threats entitled *"Mass Migration in Europe: Assimilation, Integration, and Security"*. Hungary has a clear policy position on migration therefore, let me share with you my thoughts on this very important topic that you will address this Thursday.

The way mass migration and illegal migration is handled has major implications both on the present-day situation and on the social, economic and political future of the European Union. There is an ongoing debate within the EU, which should be carried out, instead of simply dismissing certain countries' views as xenophobic, antimuslim or populist. For one, Hungary does not believe that demographic problems and/or labor shortages could be solved through migration, but rather by programs supporting families in their decision to raise more children.

Control over the external borders of the European Union is prerequisite to maintain rule of law, and the freedoms that the EU is built on, like freedom of movement within the EU. Therefore, illegal migration should be stopped. Migration must be legal, orderly and well-regulated, and mass migration is neither. Hungary, a country of ten million, encountered a massive and uncontrolled influx of illegal migrants in 2015. The long held EU hypothesis, that nobody would cross the green border illegally, went up in flames with the first wave of mass migration. Half million people crossed Hungary illegally before the Government was able to close its green borders. To put it into perspective, it is as if 12.5 million persons had entered illegally the U.S. in 2015 only. As Party to the Schengen and Dublin Agreements Hungary is under clear EU obligations to defend the external borders of the Schengen Area. This way Hungary managed to take control of the situation and divert people towards official crossings where those eligible could apply for asylum. As a result, mass migration was stopped, and illegal border crossings have dramatically decreased from thousands per day to almost zero. Foreign leaders who criticize Hungary for closing the green borders confuse human rights with humanitarian laws, and cynically negate EU obligations. There is no right for people to move across Europe unimpeded, and choose their residence as they please.

The hearing also addresses the security and public safety element of mass migration. Increased threat of terrorism and the deterioration of public security in many countries of Western Europe is now linked to uncontrolled mass migration. This link has been observed by DHS that have introduced added security measures on travel from Europe. People do not leave their beliefs, social norms, and convictions at the border either. Therefore, mass migration into other countries, undeniably alters the situation in the recipient countries. Mass migration brought rising antisemitism, physical attacks and sometimes murder of people, targeted for their Jewish religion. One cornerstone of the European social fabric and culture, that is women's equality, is endangered in certain places. Under mass migration, integration efforts crumble, putting strain on social and health care systems Bringing migrants to the labor market is harder than expected, even in the wealthiest countries. While public sentiment in Europe is largely on Hungary's side on the issue of migration, European political elites have just started to come around. Instead of recognizing their disconnect from the wishes of their electorate, some Governments still want to *punish* Hungary and others that do not want to repeat their mistakes.

Unfortunately, the European Commission is pushing for a mandatory migrant quota system. Hungary rejects that approach. The number of migrants to be settled, and also who to be accepted, is a sovereign decision of a state. The U.S. would not accept it otherwise, and nor does Hungary. Mandatory quotas for individual countries are unenforceable in the EU, as people's movement through the internal "borders" within the Schengen area is unimpeded and unchecked. Mandatory quota system without upper limits creates a pull factor, similarly to the original "Willkommenskultur", inviting more migrants to Europe. International organizations, and the EU especially, should rather focus on stemming mass migration and tackling the root causes of migration. Providing assistance to crisis zones and neighboring countries as well as fighting human trafficking are key elements. Also, contributing to the stability of originating and transit countries should be in focus. At the end of last 2017, the Visegrád Countries (Poland, Czech Republic, Slovakia and Hungary) have offered 35 MEUR to assist border protection in Libya. Hungary has boots on the ground in Iraq and in Afghanistan in our joint efforts to fight ISIS and bring stability to these regions. The Hungarian government has been a strong advocate for allocating resources to aid and reconstruction efforts in communities impacted by war, rather than importing the problems to Europe. This measured position cannot be equated with lack of compassion, intolerance and/or xenophobia.

The initiative called "Hungary Helps" brings assistance, where it is most needed. As part of that effort, Hungary has financed the reconstruction of a town on the Niniveh-plain, Tell-Asquf as well as the reconstruction of schools and hospitals and churches. Hungary spearheads the effort to assist persecuted Christians in the Middle East, so the cradle of Christianity could be preserved, and these communities could continue to exist in their homeland. Having said that, Hungary's focus is not exclusively on the plight of Christians. Just to give one example, Hungary also provides university scholarships for students from around 50 countries, nearly half of them affected by the migration crisis, e.g. Syria, Iraq, Lebanon, Kenya, Nigeria and Ethiopia. In the academic year of 2017–2018 the number of these students studying in Hungary exceeded 6,400.

Please also find attached for your perusal, two documents related to the matter, one from Századvég Foundation of Hungary, the other done by Pew Research Center in 2017.

I look forward to your thoughts on this highly relevant topic as well as new options for closer coordination and cooperation with the United States on tackling mass migration and illegal migration.

Sincerely,

László Szabó, M.D.

3910 Shoemaker Street, NW, Washington, DC 20008
Tel: (202) 362-3273, Fax: (202) 686-5580

Pew Research Center

FOR RELEASE JUNE 15, 2017

Post-Brexit, Europeans More Favorable Toward EU

But many back empowering national governments on migration and trade, and they want their own vote on EU membership

BY *Bruce Stokes, Richard Wike and Dorothy Manevich*

FOR MEDIA OR OTHER INQUIRIES:

Bruce Stokes, Director, Global Economic Attitudes
Richard Wike, Director, Global Attitudes Research
Rhonda Stewart, Senior Communications Manager

202.419.4372

www.pewresearch.org

NOTE: The preceding document has not been printed here in full but may be found at https://docs.house.gov/Committee/Calendar/ByEvent.aspx?EventID=108229

Material submitted for the record by Marta Vrbetic, Ph.D., global fellow, Global Europe Program, Woodrow Wilson International Center for Scholars

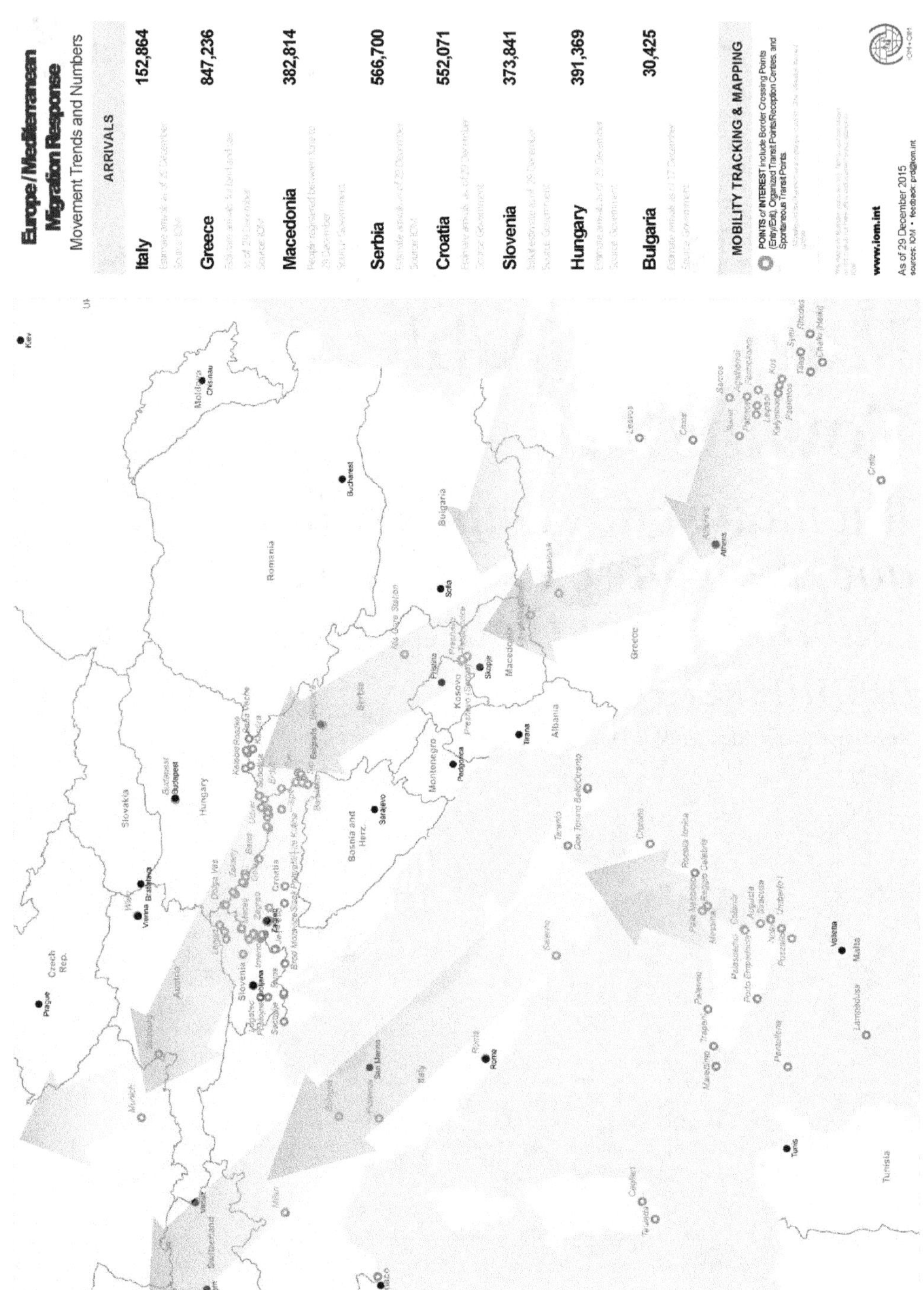

Monthly arrivals to Europe - comparison 2015, 2016 and 2017

Source: IOM, http://migration.iom.int/docs/2017_Overview_Arrivals_to_Europe.pdf

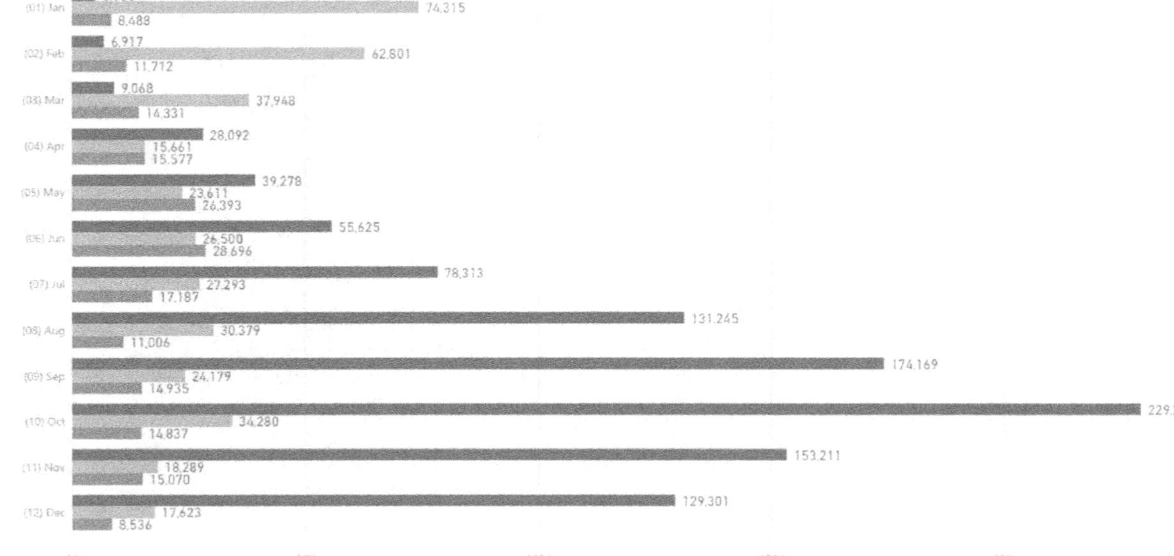

2

Map with main origin countries registered arriving to Italy and Greece in 2017 with indicated main departure points and transit routes

Source: IOM, http://migration.iom.int/docs/2017_Overview_Arrivals_to_Europe.pdf

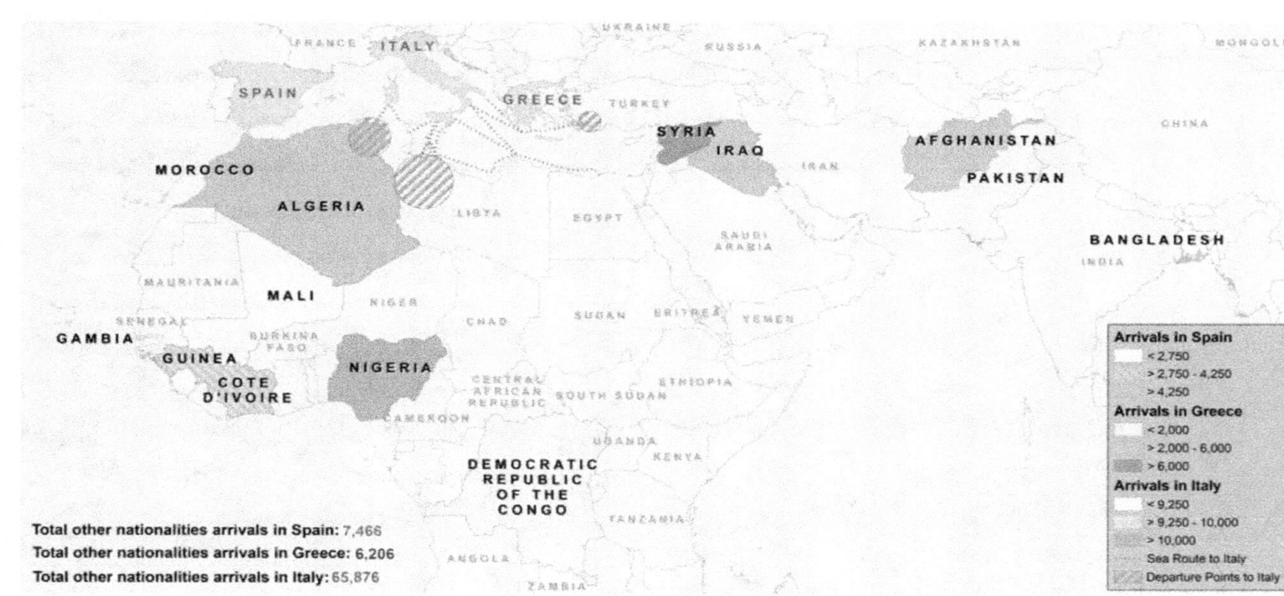

Total other nationalities arrivals in Spain: 7,466
Total other nationalities arrivals in Greece: 6,206
Total other nationalities arrivals in Italy: 65,876

International Organization for Migration (IOM)
The UN Migration Agency

MEDITERRANEAN UPDATE
MIGRATION FLOWS EUROPE: ARRIVALS AND FATALITIES

	ARRIVALS AS OF	DEATHS AS OF
ITALY	18/04/18	20/04/18
GREECE	17/04/18	20/04/18
CYPRUS	18/04/18	20/04/18
SPAIN	18/04/18	20/04/18

Asylum applications (non-EU) in the EU-28 Member States, 2006–2017(thousands)

Source: Eurostat

http://ec.europa.eu/eurostat/statistics-explained/images/1/17/Asylum_applications_%28non-EU%29_in_the_EU-28_Member_States%2C_2006%E2%80%932017%28thousands%29_YB18.png

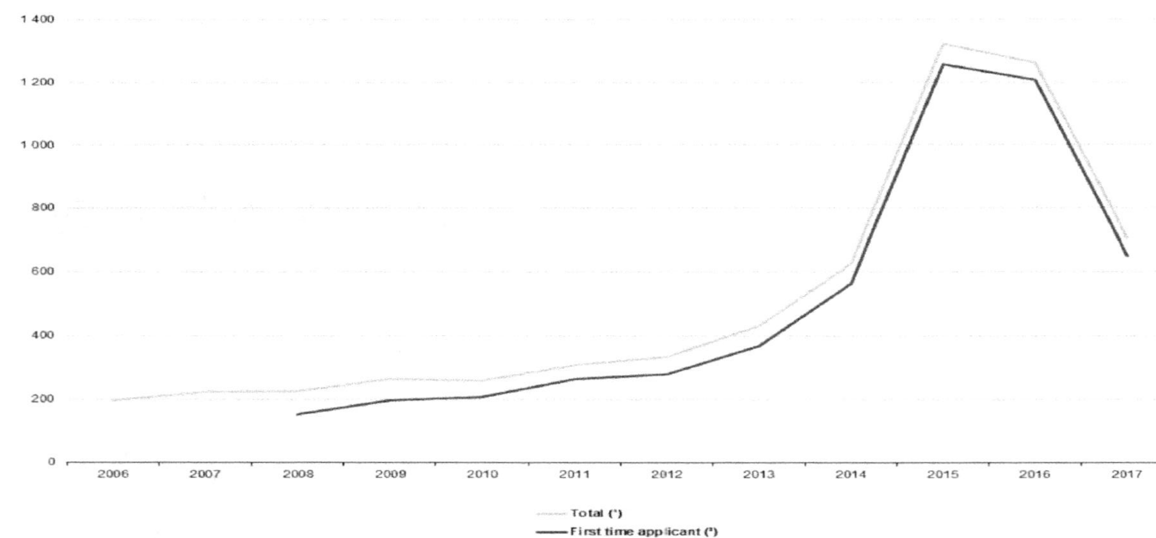

(¹) 2006 and 2007: EU-27 and extra-EU-27
(²) 2006 and 2007: not available.
Source: Eurostat (online data codes: migr_asyctz and migr_asyappctza)

Countries of citizenship of (non-EU) asylum seekers in the EU-28 Member States, 2016 and 2017 (thousands of first time applicants)
Source: Eurostat

http://ec.europa.eu/eurostat/statistics-explained/index.php?title=File:Number_of_(non-EU)_asylum_seekers_in_the_EU_and_EFTA_Member_States,_2016_and_2017_(thousands_of_first_time_applicants)_YB18.png

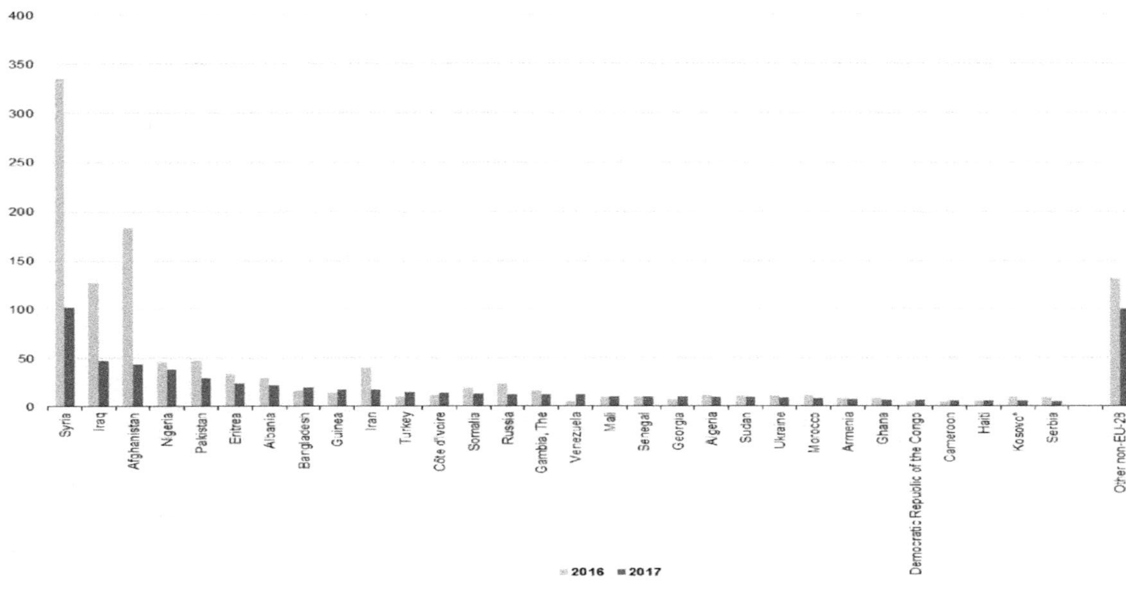

(*) This designation is without prejudice to positions on status, and is in line with UNSCR 1244/1999 and the ICJ Opinion on the Kosovo Declaration of Independence

Source: Eurostat (online data code: migr_asyappctza)

Countries of destination for asylum seekers in the EU and EFTA Member States 2016 ad 2017 (thousands of first time applicants)

Source: Eurostat

http://ec.europa.eu/eurostat/statistics-explained/index.php?title=Asylum_statistics

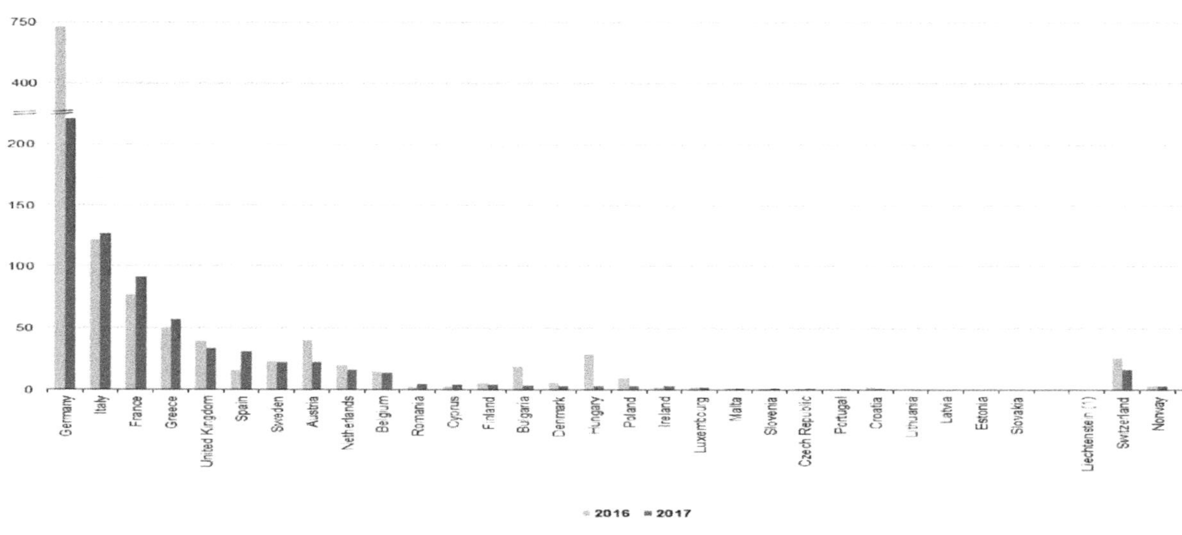

Note: the y-axis is interrupted with a different interval above the interruption from that below it.
(*) 2017: not available.
Source: Eurostat (online data code: migr_asyappctza)

www.ingramcontent.com/pod-product-compliance
Lightning Source LLC
Chambersburg PA
CBHW080035260726
48658CB00007B/2613